JB JOSSEY-BASS™
A Wiley Brand

T0319482

Gift Clubs & Societies

71 Ideas for Evaluating Your Gift Clubs
and Making Them More Inviting

Scott C. Stevenson, Editor

WILEY

For general information on our other products and services or for technical support, please contact our Customer Care Department within the United States at (800) 762-2974, outside the United States at (317) 572-3993 or fax (317) 572-4002.

Wiley publishes in a variety of print and electronic formats and by print-on-demand. Some material included with standard print versions of this book may not be included in e-books or in print-on-demand. If this book refers to media such as a CD or DVD that is not included in the version you purchased, you may download this material at http://booksupport.wiley.com. For more information about Wiley products, visit www.wiley.com.

978-1-118-69212-7   ISBN

978-1-118-70405-9   ISBN (online)

Gift Clubs & Societies
71 Ideas for Evaluating Your Gift Clubs, Making Them More Inviting

Published by

Stevenson, Inc.

P.O. Box 4528 • Sioux City, Iowa • 51104

Phone 712.239.3010 • Fax 712.239.2166

www.stevensoninc.com

Gift Clubs & Societies

71 Ideas for Evaluating Your Gift Clubs, Making Them More Inviting

TABLE OF CONTENTS

Gift Clubs & Societies
71 Ideas for Evaluating Your Gift Clubs, Making Them More Inviting

TABLE OF CONTENTS

Gift Clubs & Societies

71 Ideas for Evaluating Your Gift Clubs, Making Them More Inviting

How many giving clubs or levels do you make available to donors? Factors such as the size of your organization, size of your giving constituency and history of giving will all play into the number of gift clubs you choose to offer.

1. Giving Societies Create a Place for All Donors

Everyone knows that donor recognition is vital to donor retention. That is the motivation behind donor recognition efforts at the University of South Carolina (Columbia, SC).

"Colleges and universities should take the time to cultivate and steward donors," says Lola Mauer, director of annual giving. "Their gift is a testament to your institution and you want to ensure they remain loyal to your mission."

Offering no fewer than eight groups or societies for donors to belong to makes a statement about the appreciation the college has for its donors, Mauer says.

Some of the societies they have set up for specific groups of donors include:

✓ **Carolina Circle** — Honors donors who have made a gift for three consecutive years.

✓ **Carolina Guardian Society** — Honors donors of deferred gifts, such as trusts, bequests and annuities.

✓ **The Horseshoe Society** — Honors donors who have made cumulative gifts of $100,000 or more. There are four levels within the Horseshoe Society, based on the varying amounts of cumulative giving.

First-time donors receive a thank-you postcard introducing them to the Carolina Circle.

Eligibility for the various societies is based on annual, as well as cumulative giving, and includes corporate matches of individual gifts. These distinctions allow for inclusion into the highest annual recognition society for each donor.

With the donor recognition system in place, Mauer says, they are seeing first-time donations grow, and have more than 400 members in the Horseshoe Society and more than $14 million in matured planned gifts from the 564 members of the Carolina Guardian Society.

With donor recognition, Mauer emphasizes, the most important factor is not how you do it, but that you do it. "Whether you recognize (donors) with a special thank-you call, a postcard or a note from a student, you're showing that the investment that donor made is critical and creates opportunities for many people."

Source: Lola Mauer, Director of Annual Giving, University of South Carolina, Columbia, SC. Phone (803) 777-4092. E-mail: LMAUER@mailbox.sc.edu

Pay particular attention to those exclusive benefits you offer to donors who give at higher levels.

2. Keep an Eye on Higher-end Annual Contributions

Although it's important to do everything possible to retain all contributors from year to year, it's even more important not to lose those who give at higher levels.

Examine last year's range of giving (gift levels, gift clubs) to determine your critical gift levels. While you might have had far more contributors at the $50 - 100 level, you might discover gifts at the $1,000 - 2,500 level amounted to far more gift revenue even though there were far fewer donors in that category.

Once you have determined those gift levels that merit the most attention:

• Regularly review the names of all donors who gave at those levels to monitor who has given this year and who has yet to make a contribution.

• Have cultivation strategies in place that ensure those donors are receiving the attention they deserve throughout the year prior to being solicited for a repeat gift.

71 Ideas for Evaluating Your Gift Clubs, Making Them More Inviting

3 ## Elm Tree Society Thanks, Stewards Donors

Honor rolls, luncheons and gifts are just a few of the ways to thank and steward donors.

Staff with Scripps College (Claremont, CA) created a donor recognition society that uses those three methods and more. Currently some 300 members strong, the Elm Tree Society began in the early 1990s to honor and highlight planned giving donors and to enable the college to show its appreciation to donors through elite events and gifts.

Allyson Simpson, director of planned giving, shares the details of the society:

What are the criteria to belong to the Elm Tree Society?

"A person must have made a life-income gift (e.g., charitable gift annuity, charitable remainder trust, etc.) or have communicated a testamentary bequest intention, including the designation of the college as the beneficiary of a life insurance policy, commercial annuity or a retirement plan, such as an IRA, 401(k) or 403(b) plan."

What does the college do with the society?

"We use the society to steward existing donors, to thank and cultivate them for additional planned gifts. It has an aura of specialness about it, especially with respect to the appreciation gifts we give members, which usually bear the special society logo. This specialness also serves as an attraction for prospects we are cultivating as new planned giving donors."

What does the college do for members of the society?

"First, we feature the members prominently in the annual Honor Roll of Donors. Second, we hold at least two lunch/program events a year on campus and one or more lunch events in off-campus locations where we have a critical mass geographically of members. Usually the president of the college welcomes and thanks those in attendance at the on-campus events. Third, once a year... we present all members (in person or by mail if they cannot attend the lunch event) with a recognition gift that identifies them as society members."

Why is this society successful?

"We engage in constant, year-round stewardship and appreciation. Our members come to anticipate the events and the gifts, and seem to really enjoy both and feel good about what they have done for the future of the college."

What challenges do you face with this society? How are you overcoming them?

"Planning and executing the events and staying in touch with members who live out of the area. Because the membership is predominantly elderly, sometimes our attendance is lower than we'd like. It's difficult for some of our more elderly constituents to get to campus or the event site. We try to schedule lunch events in conjunction with other programs on campus so there will be other persons coming to campus who might be able to drive the more elderly members who do not drive anymore. We also try to match people up geographically so they can come together.... When we send gifts to out-of-area members who can't make it to campus, we always send a warm letter thanking them again for their thoughtful gift and reminding them how important they are to the future of the college."

What advice do you have for organizations interested in creating a similar society?

- "Select a name that means something to the constituent body, since planned giving is all about legacy, emotional attachment and ultimate gifts. Our name comes from the Elm Tree Lawn on campus where every commencement is held.
- "Publicize the society to existing planned giving donors and to likely planned giving prospects.
- "Steward, steward, steward on a consistent basis and show appreciation in important and visible, but relatively inexpensive, ways."

Source: Allyson Simpson, Director of Planned Giving, Scripps College, Claremont, CA. Phone (909) 621-8400. E-mail: allyson.simpson@scrippscollege.edu

Strive to make your gift clubs distinctly yours. What's unique about your organization that could tie into your gift clubs and societies?

Create Giving Options That Speak to Donors' Hearts

Boost your annual giving campaign by creating giving options that let donors follow their passions.

Doug Gortner, principal, Wessebago Consultancy (Nashville, TN), suggests setting up several distinct funds rather than one general fund. For instance, a school could ask parents to contribute to the function(s) that involve their children: Soccer parents would give to the soccer fund; theater parents would give to the theater fund, etc.

"Folks can give where their passion lies," Gortner says, "but you wouldn't be doing the duplicitous 'check the box where you want your gift applied,' knowing full well that the contributions are fungible and go into one big pot."

Offer motivation to further drive funds and staff buy-in, he says: "A key incentive would be that if gifts to a specific area exceeded budgeted expenses, those monies could be used by that sector for other legitimate expenses, such as new violins, new uniforms, new test tubes, etc."

However, he notes, an organization must be prepared to use general revenues for funds that fall short of their giving goals.

Although this alternative to a single-fund annual campaign may be more labor intensive, he says, the results are worth it.

"The donors would have an affinity to the area they are supporting, hence would be more likely to give generously and get actively involved in solicitation," Gortner says. "The rationale for fundraising would be apparent, as opposed to a commonly held attitude that the annual fund is a black hole or that you are asking for money just to ask for money."

Source: Doug Gortner, Principal, Wessebago Consultancy, Nashville, TN. Phone (615) 730-7825. E-mail: wesebago@sover.net

---

Creating Giving Categories

To establish categories within your general fund that tug at donors' hearts, Doug Gortner, principal, Wessebago Consultancy (Nashville, TN), advises:

- Establish a database capable of creating standardized reports well ahead of time.
- Survey your constituents to determine their reaction using focus groups, paper questionnaires, online surveys or interviews.
- Begin small with a modest pilot program.
- Conduct a silent campaign. Publicize its results. Before announcing the new option to give to several funds, ask key donors for leadership gifts. If a particular fund does not produce one, ask insiders to lead the way.
- Thoroughly educate constituents. "This sort of change is rife with the possibility of misinterpretation and the resulting rumors," Gortner says. To bypass this, offer a one-hour forum for employees and donors. Allow 30 minutes for questions and answers.
- Have fun, knowing that successful fundraising while stressful, is also joyous.

 Committee of 100 Generates $50,000

Want to generate more $500 gifts for your annual fund? Here's one idea:

1. Initiate an exclusive annual gift club for anyone willing to make an annual contribution of $500 and give it a name such as The Committee of 100.

2. Anyone who gives at that level gets the privilege of voting how they wish to have their donations used based on recommendations from staff. Committee members choose how they wish their donations to be spent.

3. To increase membership in your Committee of 100, send an appeal directed to a targeted group of would-be donors and/or coordinate a phonathon. In addition, host special receptions for key individuals in your community or targeted areas that include a brief program outlining the committee's goals.

If successful, your Committee of 100 will result in $50,000 in gifts directed to a funding project (or projects) that the group has collectively chosen.

To add exclusivity, some gift clubs actually limit the number of donors or members who can belong.

6 ### Renaming Your Gift Clubs?

Whether you're starting from scratch or reevaluating your charity's gift clubs or giving levels, put some thought into naming each club. The names you select for each level should possess a certain panache and connectedness to one another.

To help you select from a variety of gift club names, consider these possibilities:

- Notable individuals from your organization's past (e.g., employees, founders, board members and more — The Susan Monroe Society).

- Elements or objects akin to your organization's mission (e.g., an environmental organization might select tree-related elements: The Acorn Club, The Mighty Oak Guild, etc.)

- Nationally historic names or dates: The 1776 Society, The Order of Martin Luther King.

- Club names that convey integrity: Ambassadors, Distinguished Fellows, Diplomats.

- Physical attributes of your facilities: Eternal Fountain Alliance, Order of the Chimes, Rose Garden Society.

- Names that convey perpetuity: Legacy Fellowship, Heritage Society.

- Endearing names: Angels for Children, Lifesavers Club.

- Names tied to traditions (e.g., mascots, school colors and more: The Blue and Gold Club, Tiger Loyalists).

Put some thought into what you choose to call each gift club. What's the meaning behind it?

7 ### Publish Stories About Your Higher-end Gift Clubs

Some people are motivated to give for social reasons — they like being part of an exclusive group. Be sure to include an occasional feature about your higher-end gift clubs in your planned gifts newsletter and/or local newspaper's business or lifestyle section to let people know what it's like to be a part of such groups.

Stories could include:

✓ A profile on the club chair.

✓ Feature and photos of a recent members-only reception.

✓ Brief history of how a higher-end club got its name (list benefits).

✓ How much club members gave combined to your nonprofit.

✓ A list of higher-end club members and invitation for others to join.

✓ Reasons why businesses that are members of your higher-end club believe membership matters.

✓ A calendar of members-only events, tours, receptions and other events.

Remember to also submit to your local newspaper a story about your newly appointed board members and newly elected chairperson, along with goals for the upcoming year.

To add more meaning to them and attract new donors, make a point to draw attention to your various gift clubs and societies at various times throughout the year.

Gift Clubs & Societies

71 Ideas for Evaluating Your Gift Clubs, Making Them More Inviting

Are there any giving circles that choose to support your organization? What are you doing to attract the interest of giving circles?

8 So You Want to Host a Giving Circle.... What's Next?

Giving circles — groups of persons linked by a common desire to philanthropically support a specific organization, mission or cause, and who generally do so through a pooled fund — are growing in popularity.

Whether you have a giving circle tied specifically to your organization or not, becoming a host for one can be good for your organization, says Danielle Hicks, assistant director for new ventures in philanthropy, Forum of Regional Associations of Grantmakers (Washington, D.C.).

So how do you go about successfully hosting a giving circle? The two key ingredients, Hicks says, are support and engagement.

Providing the giving circle with both technical and administrative support is definitely helpful, she says, but thinking of ways for members to be able to contribute their time and expertise in addition to their funds is paramount.

"It's important to be really clear about what the member's expectations for the circle are and what your organization's needs are up front," she says. "Can you really use the help they're offering? Giving circle members tend to want a more personal connection to the project they're supporting, so offer opportunities for them to see the organization in action." Send regular updates on what your organization is accomplishing in general, and with regard to projects funded by the giving circle.

In closing, Hicks says, keep in mind that giving circles are generally led by volunteers, as this fact may impact your expectations about communication with the group.

Source: Danielle Hicks, Assistant Director for New Ventures in Philanthropy, Forum of Regional Associations of Grantmakers, Washington, D.C. Phone (202) 467-1131. E-mail: dhicks@givingforum.org

9 Seven Ways to Upgrade Donors' Giving

How much effort are you putting into moving current donors giving levels up? In many instances, time spent doing that will be more productive than focusing on landing new gifts.

Incorporate these strategies for upgrading contributors' gifts:

1. Secure a challenge gift that matches all gift increases of $100 or more.
2. Approach current donors for a second gift before the end of your fiscal year.
3. Enlist the help of donors in a particular gift club to call on current donors giving at lower levels.
4. Identify a special funding project that will motivate donors to give more than in previous years.
5. Conduct focus groups to reevaluate each gift club's benefits. Then publicize changes to all past contributors.
6. Emphasize quarterly and monthly pledge payments as a way to maximize giving.
7. Incorporate an annual fund theme that encourages increased giving: "7 Percent More Will Make a World of Difference!"

The benefits associated with your various giving levels can play a role in upgrading donors' support.

71 Ideas for Evaluating Your Gift Clubs, Making Them More Inviting

 ### Giving Club Revamp Emphasizes Long-term Intent

When a major fundraising tool is not as effective as it could be, consider retooling it.

Andrea Meloan, director of the Jewell Fund, William Jewell College (Liberty, MO) says their previous leadership giving society was not as effective as they would have liked. "Donors seemed too focused on the first-time member benefit (a name-inscribed brick installed in the Quadrangle, a main part of campus), and we had more lapsed leadership-level donors than we were comfortable with," Meloan says.

Development staff recognized the need for a new society that better emphasized the importance of leadership gifts to the college's annual fund over the long term — and the John Priest Greene Society was born.

This new society honors the legacy of Jewell's longest-serving president, with an eye on getting donors to make long-term commitments to the college as well. Meloan says the goal is to increase the number of donors who give at the leadership level on an annual basis. "New members join the society after they make a multi-year commitment or a sustaining (until further notice) commitment to the Jewell Fund."

John Priest Greene Society members are expected to make an annual leadership gift of at least $1,000 to the Jewell Fund, at any point during the college's fiscal year. They also refer prospective students, promote the mission of the college in their communities and encourage others to support Jewell in similar ways.

Members receive a members-only quarterly newsletter from the president, invitation to an annual president's reception and recognition in the annual Honor Roll of Donors report.

First-time leadership level donors still receive the inscribed brick on the Quad, which becomes a permanent part of Jewell —something Meloan says she hopes the donor will become too. "We worked to come up with a name for the society that would reflect what this group of people represents for the college — service and support that will have a lasting effect on strengthening Jewell for future generations."

Source: Andrea Meloan, Director of the Jewell Fund, William Jewell College, Liberty, MO. Phone (816) 415-7831. E-mail: meloana@william.jewell.edu

---

Steps to Kick Off New Gift Club

When development staff at William Jewell College (Liberty, MO) decided to replace an existing leadership giving society with one that focused on donors' long-term commitment to leadership gifts, they knew they had their work cut out for them.

Here's a look at their efforts to make the new club successful, by the numbers, six months into the process:

✓ Sent personal invitations to join from the college's president to a select group of 700 people.

✓ Had personal contacts with more than 300 recipients of the invitation.

✓ Sent the first issue of a quarterly newsletter that focuses on affirming how members' annual investments benefit the college.

✓ Have had 20 member households give at the leadership level this year, but have not yet committed to long-term giving.

✓ Have had 10 persons give at the leadership level this year, but decline membership because they could not commit to long-term giving.

✓ Confirmed 100 new members (households) to date, more than half way to their first-year goal of 150.

Your gift clubs and accompanying benefits should be evaluated on a yearly basis.

11   Put Some Thought Into Your Gift Club Names, Benefits

When was the last time you evaluated the various giving levels or clubs and accompanying benefits you offer to those donors who contribute varying amounts?

What you call each gift level and what you offer as corresponding benefits are no trivial matters. Granted, many persons will give based on other reasons, but if your gift clubs (or levels) influence even five percent of your constituents, isn't that reason enough to evaluate this aspect of your development operation?

In evaluating your gift clubs and corresponding benefits, ask these key questions:

1. **Should the names of each giving level or club be changed?** Make the names of giving levels distinctive to your organization's mission and history. Don't fall into the common century club label for those who give at the $100 level, for instance. Be creative. If that's difficult, consult a reputable ad agency for ideas or sponsor a contest to name your gift clubs.

2. **Should the gift range of each level be changed?** Analyze how many gifts you have been receiving at each level. Perhaps you have too many lower-end categories.

3. **Are the benefits offered for each giving level conducive to increasing support?** If you intend to offer benefits, make them meaningful. Even more importantly, distinguish benefits between each level to make upgrading support more compelling.

4. **How does the prestigiousness of the top giving level stand apart from all lower levels?** The benefits and distinctiveness of your top giving level should be the envy of donors at lesser levels. All constituents should perceive membership at this level to be imposing.

Develop targeted strategies aimed at increasing donors' levels of support.

12   Upgrade Donors to the Next Gift Level, Club

Rather than send a general appeal to everyone on your mailing list, here's a more targeted way of upgrading current contributors to the next gift level or club:

1. **Create a separate brochure** for each of your gift clubs that spells out the gift minimum (or gift ranges) to belong and describes donor benefits for that club. A gift club brochure should not be expensive to produce; the contents are what matter most. You could, in fact, produce a template brochure in-house and simply vary the contents to fit each club's gift ranges and accompanying benefits.

2. **Segment last year's contributors** according to the gift clubs to which they belong.

3. **Develop a personalized appeal letter** that includes the donor's name, states the gift club to which he/she currently belongs and invites the donor to upgrade his/her gift to the next gift club. Include the brochure for the upgraded gift club (along with a return envelope) with that letter.

This more targeted approach will no doubt produce more successful results than a general appeal.

71 Ideas for Evaluating Your Gift Clubs, Making Them More Inviting

13 Review Others' Top Gift Clubs to Refine Your Own

What's your organization's top giving club or level for annual gifts? How do the benefits of contributing at that level differ from lower-level giving? How do donor benefits from your top gift level differ from those of other nonprofits' most prestigious gift clubs?

Your most generous annual giving donors will obviously be top candidates when it comes to seeking major gifts. That's why it's important to keep expanding that pool. To do so, your top giving level (or club) should be perceived as one to which everyone wants to belong.

Look at the nonprofits throughout your community. Many have prestigious membership levels for those who give at, say, the $1,000-and-above level. Which nonprofits enjoy the greatest number of donors at that level? Which are perceived to be the most prestigious groups?

To refine your own top gift club, learn and evaluate what others are doing by:

1. **Picking up literature from other nonprofits** to see how they market their top gift club and determine what benefits they offer donors at that level.

2. **Finding out who, among your donor constituency, also gives generously to other nonprofit groups.** Visit with them to gain insight into their perceptions of other nonprofits' top giving groups. What do they find most appealing about them? What do they least like? What events do they make a point to attend and why?

3. **Conducting a focus group discussion** — or distributing a survey — with a handful of your donors who are presently contributing at your top level. Ask them questions that reveal perceptions about your current club benefits.

Reasons for Gift Clubs

Does your organization have giving clubs and accompanying benefits for various levels of annual support?

There are several reasons to form gift clubs or enhance existing ones. Gift clubs:

- Help motivate donors to increase their giving — raising the bar.
- Provide a sense of belonging to those who make contributions.
- Serve as a way to recognize donors' gifts (by listing their names in annual reports and elsewhere).
- Help in identifying major gift prospects — those in your top level.
- Provide a means for offering increased benefits as gifts increase.

---

14 Create a Menu of Upgrading Approaches

How do you go about asking a past contributor for an increased gift? Do you have more than one approach? It makes sense to develop a menu of approaches from which to choose as you work to upgrade past donors' gifts.

Here are some examples to use as a guide in preparing your upgrade menu of asks based on:

Fiscal year goal — "This year's annual fund goal is 10 percent higher than what was raised last year. That's why we're asking everyone to consider a 10 percent increase in their giving."

Gift clubs — "You're only $50 shy of being included in the next-higher gift club. I want to invite you to be a part of that group."

Cost of providing services — "It's expected that the cost of providing the same level of services as last year will increase by 6 percent. If everyone can increase their giving by that amount or more, we can keep pace with what's been done in the past."

Additional projects — "I recognize and appreciate what you have already contributed this year, but it wouldn't be fair to you not to tell you about this special project that we're attempting to fund by year's end."

As you develop a menu of upgrading asks, be sure to incorporate gift club benefits into your mix.

71 Ideas for Evaluating Your Gift Clubs, Making Them More Inviting

 15 Analyze Year's Worth of Giving by Levels, Clubs

How much attention do you pay to gift results as they relate to giving levels or clubs? Analyzing those results annually can help identify ways to enhance your organization's fundraising strategies. See analysis graph, below.

If, for instance, you see significant growth in a particular level or club, you may choose to focus more fundraising strategies on that level. Or if a club is not living up to expectations, you may decide it's time to revamp its benefits or take other actions.

Knowing each level's total donors, gift amount and how gifts were solicited can help you to make more informed decisions regarding future fundraising strategies.

2010 GIVING BASED ON CLUB LEVELS

Club/ Group	Gift Range	No. Donors/ % of Total	Total Gifts	% of Total Dollars	Direct Mail	Tele- solicitation	Personal Calls
J. Doe Club	$5,000-plus	18 (2%)	$147,000	44.0%	None	1 (5.5%)	17 (94.4%)
Gold Circle	$1,000-4,999	34 (4%)	78,500	23.6%	6 (17.6%)	2 (5.8%)	26 (76.4%)
Benefactors	$500-999	65 (7.6%)	41,200	12.4%	12 (18.4%)	4 (6.1%)	49 (75.3%)
Patrons	$100-499	218 (25.5%)	38,900	11.7%	171 (78.4%)	41 (18.8%)	6 (2.7%)
Friends	Up to $99	517 (60.7%)	25,850	7.8%	344 (66.5%)	156 (30%)	17 (3.3%)
		852	$331,450		533	204	115

 16 Giving Society Celebrates Consistent Donor Support

At Agnes Scott College (Decatur, GA), gift size takes a back seat to donor loyalty when it comes to recognition.

The college's Fideles Society recognizes donor loyalty without regard to the amount of giving, emphasizing that every gift counts, says Joanne Davis, director of the annual fund. College officials, Davis says, were looking for an incentive to encourage donors to give each year, "and we were also looking for a way to recognize donors no matter what size their gift, knowing that not everyone can make large gifts."

Thus, the Fideles Society was born.

Today, at just three years of age, the society boasts more than 3,000 members. Here's how the program works:

Donors who give to the annual fund for three consecutive years become members of the Fideles Society, regardless of the amount of those gifts. Members receive a car decal with the Fideles Society logo and have an "F" by their name in the annual report.

Members receive a spring mailing encouraging them to give to maintain their membership. Phonathon callers also have a record of the alumna's giving and are able to remind society members that a gift will maintain their membership.

College officials are also considering designing a new decal to celebrate five-year members of the society.

Benefits to the college are obvious, she says. "It gives us a strong nucleus of donors we can depend on year after year. For the past seven years our alumnae participation has averaged between 42 and 47 percent."

Before embarking on a similar project, Davis recommends, make sure giving records are accurate and talk to other charities with similar recognition programs.

Source: Joanne Davis, Director of the Annual Fund, Agnes Scott College, Decatur, GA. Phone (404) 471-5343. E-mail: jadavis@agnesscott.edu

The goal of some gift clubs is to encourage donors to give consecutively over a period of years.

71 Ideas for Evaluating Your Gift Clubs, Making Them More Inviting

17 **Designing a Recognition Society, What to Consider**

Designing a recognition society requires much more than coming up with a meaningful name and attractive benefits. "You'll also need to decide what you want to accomplish and what is manageable for your organization," says Judith T. Davis, marketing associate for gift planning, Virginia Tech (Blacksburg, VA).

Davis shares questions to discuss to help design a workable recognition society:

- How many members can our organization effectively recognize; how often?
- Will we recognize individuals only or include corporations?
- How will we handle joint gifts and household giving (including giving by unmarried couples in the same household)?
- How will we count gifts made by parent-members and credited to a son or daughter in order to gain membership for the son or daughter?
- How will we handle membership for spouses whose combined giving qualifies for membership, but who divorce, leaving one or both below necessary giving level?
- Will we count matching gifts?
- Will we count gifts in kind; at what value?
- Will we count pledges; how will we handle pledges that are not honored?
- How will we handle gifts for which there is a quid pro quo (e.g., season tickets)?
- Will we count deferred giving/estate gift commitments; how will they be valued?
- Will we require documentation for estate gift commitments?
- Will we need a separate deferred giving society; will members qualify regardless of gift value?
- What benefits of membership do we want to offer; how are these benefits meaningful to the donors; can the benefits be sustained?
- Will we do something special for charter members?
- Will we have a single-level giving society, tiered levels within one society, or multiple societies?
- Will we offer those nearing a tier threshold an opportunity to make an additional gift to advance to the next level? How will we notify them; recognize them?
- What annual deadlines will be needed for new members to qualify in time to participate in an event or be listed on an honor roll?
- What specific staff member will be responsible for approving an offer of membership before it is made, and who will sign the offer letter?
- What will prompt a membership offer (e.g., every time a giving report is produced; only when you run a special report)?
- How and when will we communicate with development officers about membership offers and advancements for their donors?
- When listing members, how will we balance consistent listing and donor preferences (e.g., will you use titles such as Dr. always, never, on request; use nicknames; list alumnus first; list wife or husband first; etc.)?
- How many levels of anonymous will we have (e.g., always; anonymous when gift ranges are mentioned; whenever specific amounts are mentioned; etc.)?
- How will we confirm donor preferences such as anonymity (e.g., a questionnaire with a limited menu of options; personal conversation; etc.)?
- How will we indicate membership, anonymity, induction date or other information on the database?
- How will we indicate in our database that a qualified person declined membership?

Source: Judith T. Davis, Marketing Associate for Gift Planning, University Development, Virginia Tech, Blacksburg, VA. Phone (540) 231-2279. E-mail: judithb@vt.edu

Considering a new gift club or recognition society? Here are a few of the questions you should answer during that planning process.

18 Create a Special Club for Business Contributors

If generating more support from businesses is a key goal, consider a special gift club, or bolstering your existing club. Just like individuals, businesses, too, like being part of an exclusive group. Consider giving businesses that make a minimum annual gift:

- Tickets to some of your events throughout the year.
- Invitations to join a special business advisory group.
- Invitations to a series of programs throughout the year geared specifically to business interests — monthly business executives' breakfast, speakers' program, etc.
- Inclusion of its name in a special section of your annual honor roll of contributors.
- A special rate on some service(s) provided by your organization.
- A personal visit by your organization's CEO and/or board chair.
- A plaque, certificate or other memento to display as a proud supporter of your cause.

Give Business Donors Special Status

Create a program tailored to attracting financial support from local and area businesses.

One East Coast university created The Ambassador Club to recognize businesses giving $500 or more a year. Members attend events geared to them. Gifts have grown significantly as a result of the focused effort.

Make a yearlong commitment to host monthly events that include a brief program on topics geared to the interests of attendees. Form an advisory committee to identify and offer perks that grab the attention of would-be members.

---

19 Play on Gift Clubs' Attraction as Status Symbols

As a donor, being associated with a major giving club can rightly bring a sense of pride.

As a development office, being aware of that element can help determine how — and to whom — to market such giving options.

The five major gift clubs offered at Clemson University (Clemson, SC) provide incentives for giving, says Ann Batson Smith, director of annual giving.

"Having gift clubs at all levels is a motivator for people to increase their gifts," says Batson Smith. "There is a certain status symbol for a donor to say they give at a major gift club level."

The annual major gift club levels offered at Clemson include:

- ✓ President's Club ($1,000 to $2,499) with 1,440 members;
- ✓ Clemson Ambassadors ($2,500 to $4,999) with 265 members;
- ✓ Clemson Fellows ($5,000 to $9,999) with 193 members;
- ✓ Founders ($10,000 to $24,999) with 200 members; and
- ✓ Heritage Partners ($25,000 or more), with 130 members.

"Donors at the major gift club level do feel there is a status associated with giving at the major giving level," Batson Smith says. "I believe they expect a certain exclusivity, so we try to send them special messages from the president or leadership groups, special invitations to major gift club events and sometimes earlier notification of campus news."

While gift clubs are great incentives to give at a higher level, Batson Smith recommends planning for increased costs associated with stewarding this group of donors while staying within Internal Revenue Service guidelines for the amount of benefits these donors receive if your organization allows a 100 percent tax-deductible gift.

Source: Ann Batson Smith, Director of Annual Giving, Clemson University, Clemson, SC. Phone (864) 656-5895. E-mail: annsmit@clemson.edu

If your organization has a long history of giving and a constituency of higher-end donors, you might want to consider having multiple higher-end gift clubs.

71 Ideas for Evaluating Your Gift Clubs, Making Them More Inviting

20 Beef Up Your Top Gift Club

To attract more major gifts, build your base of top level annual gifts. To do so, first evaluate your top gift level or gift club. Is it sufficiently exclusive? Are its benefits compelling? Do members get the recognition they deserve?

Whether entry into your top annual gift level begins with a gift of $1,000 or $100,000, here are ideas to beef up the value of this critical group:

1. In addition to one brochure that describes each of your gift clubs, design a special brochure for your top gift category. List membership benefits and previous year's donors.

2. Select a recognized and respected individual (or individuals) to chair your top club each year. Utilize the chair's signature on special communications and appeals, and ask the chair(s) to help host special events for this prestigious group.

3. Select a name for the top club that sets it apart from other giving levels: The Society of... The President's Guild... The Order of...

4. Coordinate a special recognition event each year that inducts new donors into the club or society.

5. Host receptions throughout the year, some for members only, others that encourage members to bring prospective members as guests.

6. Present new members with a plaque or some other item that can have name plates added to it for subsequent years' gifts.

7. Recognize donors at this level distinctively in your annual honor roll of contributors. List the number of consecutive years at this level next to each donor's name.

8. Provide club members with invitations to special events held throughout the year.

9. Ask club members to stand and be recognized at public events.

10. Provide members with special perks (e.g., special parking, seating).

11. Have your CEO send all donors at this level personal notes of appreciation and periodic updates.

12. Introduce club members at a board meeting.

Work to beef up your top giving clubs.

21 Create Lifetime Society to Honor Noteworthy Donors

While creating gift clubs based on annual giving amounts is a smart idea, going beyond those expected parameters to establish an exclusive society can serve to intrigue, and ultimately attract, major donors.

Consider the possibility of an exclusive lifetime society that also recognizes all donors who give at an extraordinarily high level. For example, anyone who makes a gift — outright, planned or a combination thereof — of $100,000 or more gets inducted into a special lifetime society that includes certain benefits.

Make admittance to this exclusive group a formal induction process with accompanying benefits.

A lifetime club such as this doesn't discourage future giving, yet it does collectively recognize those whose level of support is consequential.

One of the most exclusive giving clubs offers lifetime memberships as a benefit.

71 Ideas for Evaluating Your Gift Clubs, Making Them More Inviting

 22 | **Start a Consecutive-year Giving Recognition Program**

If you would like more donors to give consistently over time, consider starting a consecutive giving program that recognizes those donors.

Why not launch a program that recognizes all donors who have given consecutively (year-after-year) for five years or more. The program would not only serve to recognize these donors but also help to retain and motivate others to give more consistently.

Establish a committee to oversee, name and identify member perks for the club. Select the committee's membership from among those who already have a record of consistent giving.

The Order of the Emerald

The Order of the Emerald recognizes those loyal supporters who have given consecutively for five or more years.

20 or More Years of Giving

Henry Gladstone	Mr./Mrs. Alvin Gotland	Acme Paint

10 to 19 Years of Giving

Rochett Manufacturing	Mr./Mrs. Merl Arends	Lonnie George

6 to 9 Years of Giving

Larry Emmers	Mr./Mrs. Tim Harms	Dr./Mrs. Mike Nob
Sally Fertig	Tom and Mary Jacobs	Dan Otter

5 Years of Giving

Mitchell Andrews	Mr./Mrs. Al Jacobs	Lois Simms
Mark & Ellen Barry	Joan Newcomb	Richard Utze

---

 23 | **Society Gives Young Alums Stepping Stone to Gifts**

Did you hear the one about the recent college graduate rolling in dough? Neither did we.

Fact is, most recent grads don't have lots of money — some might not even have a job. So bringing these people into your donor fold takes patience and special care.

Carrie Moore, assistant director, donor relations, Texas Christian University (Fort Worth, TX), says their Junior Clark Society is one way they have found to engage young alums and help them move, slowly, up the ladder to major giving.

Based on the university's existing Clark Society, which gives special benefits to those pace-setting donors who make a gift of $1,000 or more, the Junior Clark Society uses a tiered system of giving to help build younger donors up to a major giving level.

In the first three years following graduation, Junior Clark members make an annual gift of $100. In years four through six, they make an annual gift of $300. Finally, in years seven through nine, they make an annual gift of $500.

The hope is that as their careers grow, so too will their incomes and the donations they are able to make to TCU. Ideally, by the time they hit year 10, annual giving will have become such a habit they will continue making gifts to the university.

For their participation, members receive an invitation to a Clark Society Weekend and other campus events, library privileges globally accessible via the Internet, recognition in TCU publications, a Junior Clark car decal and the opportunity to network with some of TCU's most successful alums.

Those who give $750 or more designated to the Frog Fan Club also receive a named, reserved parking space for TCU's home Horned Frog football games, and the university gets the chance to make lifelong donors out of some of TCU's biggest fans.

The Junior Clark Society currently has approximately 250 members.

Source: Carrie Moore, Assistant Director, Donor Relations, Texas Christian University, Fort Worth, TX. Phone (817) 257-6965. E-mail: cmoore2@tcu.edu

Do you have a club that's aimed at attracting younger individuals to establish a habit of giving?

71 Ideas for Evaluating Your Gift Clubs, Making Them More Inviting

 Consider a Yearly Operational Plan Based On Giving Levels

There are many ways of creating a yearly operational plan complete with goals, quantifiable objectives and action plans. One way of doing that is to use your gift clubs or levels as the foundation, creating strategies that attract new contributors at each level and moving current donors up the giving ladder.

Development shops that use these gift clubs as the centerpiece of their yearly operational planning should identify quantifiable objectives and accompanying action plans for each gift level. This allows the development team to allocate time and resources more appropriately, with prospects at the lowest gift level receiving the least amount of time and resources and those at the top end receiving the most attention.

Review the accompanying operational plan objectives as a way to understand how gift clubs can become the focus of planning.

2010-11 Operational Plan Objectives

The President's Guild — Annual Contributors of $5,000 and above

Objectives
1. To host the annual President's Guild Dinner.
2. To create a yearly cultivation/solicitation plan for each member of The President's Guild.
3. To personally call on and renew each President's Guild member.
4. To provide special seating for President's Guild members at the annual Gala.
5. To invite all members to the quarterly Susan Haines Society receptions.
6. To increase the number of new Guild members by 2 percent.

Susan Haines Society — Annual Contributors of $1,000 to $4,999

Objectives
1. To host quarterly receptions for members of the Susan Haines Society.
2. To personally call on and renew all current Susan Haines Society members.
3. To personally cultivate and invite no less than 20 percent of Susan Haines Society members to join The President's Guild.
4. To encourage all current Society members (through various means) to enlist one new member.
5. To increase the number of new Susan Haines Society members by 3 percent.

The Emerald Club — Annual Contributors of $500 to $999

Objectives
1. To identify those Emerald Club members who should be solicited through face-to-face calls.
2. To direct two personalized renewal letters to Emerald Club members who are not seen face-to-face.
3. To invite no less than 40 percent of Emerald Club members to become Susan Haines Society members.
4. To increase the number of new Emerald Club members by 3 percent.

The League of Ridgemont — Annual Contributors of $100 to $499

Objectives
1. To identify those League members who should be personally contacted.
2. To renew all current League members through the annual phonathon and/or direct mail appeals.
3. To invite no less than 30 percent of League members to contribute at The Emerald Club level.
4. To increase the number of new League members by 4 percent.

Ridgemont Members — Annual Contributions of Less Than $100

Objectives
1. To renew all Ridgemont members through direct mail, the annual phonathon or personal calls.
2. To invite no less than 50 percent of Ridgemont members to contribute at the League of Ridgemont level.
3. To increase the number of new Ridgemont members by 10 percent.

Gift Clubs & Societies

71 Ideas for Evaluating Your Gift Clubs, Making Them More Inviting

Sometimes naming a gift club after someone with strong ties to your organization helps draw support.

25 Gift Clubs Boost Bottom Line

Gift clubs can really boost your bottom line. Just ask Vicki McNamara, executive director, Warren County United Way, Inc. (Monmouth, WI). Their gift clubs boast more than 260 members, raising an additional $60,000 in funds annually.

Here's how the gift clubs are set up:

1. Len G. Everett Society ($1,000 and above) — Named for a local artist who funded an endowment that currently covers 100 percent of the organization's administrative costs, this society recognizes the community's deeply rooted tradition of giving.

2. The President's Club ($500-$999) — Representing the spirit of neighbor helping neighbor, this club was founded to involve and deepen the understanding, commitment and support of the community's leadership.

3. The Leadership Club ($300-$499) —Members of this club know they are partnering to fulfill the community's human needs with their gift.

The United Way chapter also has seven levels of leadership recognition for donors who give through their company's annual campaign.

When setting up gift clubs, says McNamara, look at different club levels in relation to your metro area, then try to implement something that works in that environment.

Source: Vicki McNamara, Executive Director, Warren County United Way, Inc., Monmouth, OH. Phone (309)734-6364. E-mail: wcunitedway@juno.com

26 Give High-end Contributors Deserved Recognition

How do you set apart higher-end annual contributors — say those who give $1,000 or more — from the rest of your organization's supporters?

It's important you give these donors the recognition they deserve, especially knowing they will be the ones you count on for major gifts if/when you launch a major fundraising effort.

Evaluate the ways in which you distinguish this important group of annual contributors from others. Your recognition efforts may include:

*   Giving prominent attention to these major donors in your annual honor roll of contributors.

*   Providing special seating, corsages, boutonnieres or other stand-apart recognition at particular events.

*   Making greater effort to convey the impact of their generous support to them and the community at various times throughout the year.

*   Acknowledging their gifts in more personalized ways, such as phone calls, letters, visits and other gestures from your CEO and board members.

*   Offering particular gift club benefits deemed more exclusive than those at lower levels.

Make the Most of Your $1,000-plus Reception

Whenever you're fortunate enough to assemble a large portion of your $1,000-and-above donors, make the most of the opportunity. For example, get a group photograph of everyone for use in next year's marketing literature.

71 Ideas for Evaluating Your Gift Clubs, Making Them More Inviting

 27 Make Gift and Member Club Names Distinctive

What are the names of your various gift clubs or membership levels? How long have they been in existence?

If the names of your gift clubs or membership levels are as boring as many seem to be — Century Club, President's Club, etc. — it may be time for an overhaul. After all, these various levels are created to entice donors/members, not oppress them.

Get together with staff first and then your development or membership committee. Identify several distinctive possibilities based on the various levels of support and accompanying benefits.

As you brainstorm possibilities, consider these naming options:

1. The name of an individual who made a significant difference in the life of your organization — former employee, board member, donor. Example: The Hawthorn Society.

2. Names unique to your organization's purpose or mission. Examples:

   - For an orchestra — The Quintet Club, The Symphonic Society, etc.
   - For an environmental organization — The Oak Tree Guild, The Acorn Alliance, etc.

3. Names unique to your community or region.

4. Names tied to a point in history or the history of your organization.

In addition to being distinctive, club or membership level names should be the right fit with each increasing level.

> Are the names of each of your gift clubs or giving societies distinctive? Use renaming opportunities as a way to draw attention to your club or society.

28 What's in a Name?

What do you call each of your gift clubs or levels? Is there meaning behind the names of each? Could it be time that you rethink, perhaps rename some of those gift clubs?

Be creative. Come up with names that distinguish your nonprofit from others. Here's a sampling of various gift club names used throughout the nation, some of them based on people or unique features of those nonprofits:

- ❑ Statesmen's Circle
- ❑ Circle of Care
- ❑ Founders' Club
- ❑ Century Club
- ❑ Life Member
- ❑ President's Club
- ❑ Partner
- ❑ Court of Sponsors
- ❑ Associate
- ❑ Legacy Society
- ❑ Golden Circle
- ❑ Patrons of....
- ❑ Vanguard
- ❑ Landmark Society
- ❑ Gallery of Benefactors
- ❑ Red & Gold Club (school colors)
- ❑ Ash Hall Society (first building)
- ❑ Bulldog Club (mascot)
- ❑ Deans' Circle
- ❑ Gifts of Hope
- ❑ Heritage Society
- ❑ 1896 Society (nonprofit's founding)
- ❑ Keystone
- ❑ Cornerstone Guard
- ❑ Regent's Circle
- ❑ John Alder Circle (historical figure)
- ❑ Red Wagon Club (unique story)
- ❑ Pacesetters

> Leave no stone unturned as you explore possible names for your gift clubs.

29 Hold an Annual Event for Higher-end Donors

Do you host an annual event for donors who give at the $1,000-and-above level? If enough of your contributors live within driving distance, such an event should be a must. It's a great recognition approach for several reasons, including:

1. Getting a majority of your heavy hitters together under the same roof so they can see who's in their company.

2. Providing a form of recognition that can set your organization apart from others.

3. Encouraging habitual giving at that level.

4. Offering a forum to convey key messages.

5. Motivating others who don't give at that level to begin doing so.

Whether it's a five-course meal or an opulent reception or a program with a guest celebrity speaker, be sure to do it right. Don't let lack of budget prevent you from providing a first-class event. If budget's an issue, find donors or sponsors to underwrite the cost of the affair. It's an important investment.

Generate a Planning Checklist for Your Annual Recognition Event

To plan for an exceptional recognition event, prepare a checklist of tasks or items to be included. Use the example below as a launching point:

- ❏ Event theme
- ❏ Guest list
- ❏ Invitations
- ❏ Recruit emcee
- ❏ Recruit committee
- ❏ Enlist volunteers
- ❏ Event location
- ❏ Guest welcome table
- ❏ Signs listing donors
- ❏ Dinner menu
- ❏ Printed programs listing donors
- ❏ Program agenda
- ❏ Entertainment
- ❏ Special awards
- ❏ Secure sponsors/underwriters
- ❏ Special guests
- ❏ Key remarks
- ❏ Seating arrangements
- ❏ Decorations
- ❏ Parking
- ❏ AV equipment needs

---

30 Four Ways to Evaluate Your Gift Club Benefits

Are your membership benefits (or gift clubs) all that they can be? Do the benefits you offer really motivate giving at each level? To analyze your member benefits and make needed improvements, complete any or all four of these measures:

1. **Conduct surveys of each member (or club) classification** and ask contributors at those levels to share their perceptions. Word questions to determine the roll each benefit played in motivating them to give at that level.

2. **Conduct focus groups** with a sampling of members in each gift level, asking which benefits they most value. Conduct a brainstorming session to determine what new or enhanced benefits they would most value.

3. **Chat one-on-one with lapsed contributors in each gift level** to determine why they stopped giving. What roll did club benefits play in their decisions? (Involving lapsed contributors in this process may serve to bring some of them back on board.)

4. **Look beyond your competition to see what benefits are being offered by other nonprofit organizations.** If, for instance, you represent a hospital, explore what colleges or museums or art centers are offering contributors at various gift levels. You may be able to identify and adapt some creative benefits to your charity.

To properly evaluate your gift club benefits, make a point to seek your donors' opinions, even lapsed donors.

71 Ideas for Evaluating Your Gift Clubs, Making Them More Inviting

31 How to Get on the Radar Screen of Giving Circles

A 2006 Forum of Regional Associations of Grantmakers study reports giving circles — a group of individuals (as few as five or as may as 400) who pool their money and decide together where to give it — are an enduring and expanding philanthropic trend.

The 2006 study "More Giving Together: The Growth & Impact of Giving Circles & Shared Giving," a follow-up to the association's 2004 study, identified 400 circles (50 percent more than in 2004) and collected detailed information from 160 of them.

Tailor Approach to Individual Giving Circle

Getting a giving circle's attention can be a challenge as each circle is different. Some work like a traditional foundation, in which an organization fills out a grant application, while others seek out organizations they want to fund and do not accept unsolicited proposals. Like most grantmaking bodies, a giving circle will have specific granting guidelines that can normally be found on a giving circle's website, or may be determined by looking at what type of organizations it has funded in the past.

Giving Circle of HOPE Caters to Small, Grassroots Groups

Giving Circle of HOPE (Reston, VA) specializes in small (under $2 million budget), local, grassroots organizations where its grants of $5,000 will make a difference. Organizations apply on the giving circle's website (http://givingcircleofhope.org), which also spells out what the circle will and won't fund.

"Our giving circle wanted to spread the wealth and fund as many organizations as we could any given year," says Linda Strup, co-founder and giving circle member. "We establish close relationships with our grantees and often provide volunteer help," she says. "We felt that just funding one organization per year might discourage a long-term relationship and also may encourage new projects with a pile of money but then leave them unfunded." Plus, they felt they could appeal to more potential members by not narrowing their focus too much.

Circle members invite organizations they know to apply for grants and e-mail organizations that they learn about from nonprofit forums, chamber events, newspaper articles, etc. "We network quite a bit," she says. "Some of the grant applications come from organizations we've never heard of, and we're happy about that too! One of our missions is to educate ourselves about the needs in our community, and we are glad to learn about new nonprofits and how they try to help others."

Washington Area Foundation Oversees Two Philanthropic Groups

Washington Area Women's Foundation (Washington, D.C.) oversees two giving circles — the African American Women's Giving Circle, and Rainmakers.

The Rainmakers circle solicits requests for proposals, putting the burden on the circle to get information to potential grantees, says Carolee Summer-Sparks, foundation senior program officer. They send information out by e-mail, work with other foundations, advertise in the Chronicle of Philanthropy, and work with the Forum of Regional Associations of Grantmakers to let people know they seek proposals.

The African American Women's Giving Circle seeks nonprofits to fund, calling an organization and asking specific questions, Summer-Sparks says. "They build relationships with organizations they are seeking to fund." The circle does not take unsolicited grant applications but allows organizations to send information about themselves, which is kept in a database at the Women's Foundation.

Getting funded by other foundations will also put you on giving circles' radar because they tend to look at what other foundations and giving circles are funding.

Getting a giving circle's attention can sometimes be a challenge as each circle is different. Look at the types of organizations it has funded in the past.

Sources: Linda Strup, Co-founder and Guiding Circle Member, Giving Circle of HOPE, Reston, VA. E-mail: givingcircle@hotmail.com
Carolee Summers-Sparks, Senior Program Officer, Washington Area Women's Foundation, Washington D.C. Phone (202) 347-7737, ext. 213. E-mail: lkays@wawf.org

32 Analyze Gift Club Members' Potential

Do you ever analyze individual gift clubs to strategize ways to increase giving or to encourage members to move up to the next gift level?

Doing so makes sense. But as you evaluate a particular gift club's membership, take time to also review and rate each member within that club to determine who has the greatest potential for increasing his/her gift support. That way, you can focus solicitation time on the greatest likelihood for success, based on both gift capability and inclination to give.

33 Donor Association Creates Multi-million-dollar Circle

Wonder if it's possible to raise $1 million a year with a letter-writing campaign? Ronald Guziak, executive director, Hoag Hospital Foundation (Newport Beach, CA), says its Circle 1000 cancer center support group has done so for three years running.

Circle 1000 was founded following Hoag's $23-million Patty and George Hoag Cancer Center capital campaign. The campaign raised $25 million with the help of a small committee of women. At campaign end, those women said they would like to keep raising funds for the cancer center without planning an event, and Circle 1000 was born. Members make an annual gift without a corresponding obligation to join a committee, attend meetings or events.

Since that time, Circle 1000 has raised another $9 million-plus, with many donors committing annually and steadily increasing the amount they are giving.

Each fall, the 24-woman committee holds a letter-writing campaign asking friends and associates to give a minimum of $1,500. That gift is their sole commitment and obligation for the year.

From 300 to 400 people commit to Circle 1000 annually.

Each spring, donors are invited to the Circle 1000 Founders' Brunch to hear a well-known cancer survivor. Past speakers include Scott Hamilton, Linda Ellerbee and Harry Belafonte.

Guziak says the foundation does not proactively market for Circle 1000, and notes that the cancer center speaks for itself: "The cancer center has done a great job of growing and improving as a community resource and people see that. There is a very clear, direct benefit of the money they give."

He notes that the choice of committee members makes a huge difference for the success of such a giving club. "You have to find people with passion who want to make a difference and are willing to stand up and lead."

Source: Ronald Guziak, Executive Director, Hoag Hospital Foundation, Newport Beach, CA. Phone (949) 764-7219. E-mail: Rguziak@hoaghospital.org

High-end Annual Gifts: Bring Together $1,000-plus Donors

What benefits are you offering those loyal supporters who give $1,000 or more on an annual basis?

One such benefit should be an invitation to at least one special event that celebrates their support while also drawing attention to the importance of giving at such a generous level.

Creating such an annual (or bi-annual or quarterly) event helps to convey your organization's recognition and appreciation of donors who give at that level. And equally important, it helps elevate the exclusivity of giving at these higher levels, motivating others to increase their giving to join the higher ranks.

71 Ideas for Evaluating Your Gift Clubs, Making Them More Inviting

34 Symphony Reaches Out to Physicians

Look for ways to bring together like-minded individuals for the benefit of your cause.

The Physicians for the Phoenix Symphony was formed 22 years ago by a group of symphony patrons from the medical community who wanted to take a leadership role in recognizing The Phoenix Symphony (Phoenix, AZ) as an important cultural resource.

"The group continues to sponsor concerts, hold fundraising events and private recitals, and share their enjoyment of symphonic music," says Frank E. Bourget, director of development.

The 60-member volunteer group, led by a chair and a six- to eight-person executive committee, meets monthly to discuss recruitment strategies and plan events. Members are recruited through personal contact, networking, the symphony website and event publicity.

Members' dues range from $50 to $1,500 annually, and several members give additional annual fund gifts of $10,000.

"The Physicians for the Phoenix Symphony has helped in the cultivation of major gifts by introducing us to new major gift prospects who became more involved with the symphony by attending our events, attending more concerts and becoming new annual donors and season series subscribers," says Bourget. One member, he notes, even secured a $25,000 gift from the corporation he worked for to sponsor a concert.

Members of the group organized several cultivation events in October and November 2008, including a pre-concert reception and a recital at a private home. A private concert at Steinway of Phoenix, and a salon concert at a private home, raised $5,000 each.

"Gifts usually result after further contact by major gifts staff, who make follow-up calls or send notes to people they engaged with at the event," says Bourget.

Source: Frank E. Bourget, Director of Development, The Phoenix Symphony, Phoenix, AZ. Phone (602) 452-0420. E-mail: fbourget@phoenixsymphony.org

Some gift clubs reach out to like-minded individuals or specific professions.

35 Cultivate Affinity Groups Among Your $1,000-plus Donors

If your organization is fortunate to have many $1,000-plus annual gift donors, you may wish to evaluate the group's makeup to determine how you can better cultivate existing affinity groups within that giving club or level.

Targeted cultivation aimed at particular groups will serve to retain their membership from year to year and also help in attracting new donors. Criteria such as age, occupation, gender, geographic residency and so forth should be considered in grouping donors to maximize cultivation activities. For instance, if women represent a high percentage of your $1,000-plus donors, you may develop a yearlong series of activities directed toward that group. Likewise, if many of your donors include small businesses, consider hosting regularly scheduled activities that would appeal to them.

It's important to get beyond the treat all $1,000-plus donors the same mentality that has pervaded many charities in the past.

Get to know those who make up your higher-end gift clubs. Doing so may offer clues to enhance their giving.

36 **Set Yearly Gift Club Goals**

As you set your yearly fundraising goal, get specific. Set goals for each giving level or gift club. How many new $1,000 gifts do you intend to secure for that giving level? By what percentage will contributions to your $100 to $250 gift level increase next year?

Breaking down a yearly fundraising goal helps define specific actions you will need to take to achieve it.

37 **'Discovery' Encourages Women's Philanthropy**

Ball State University (Muncie, IN) established "Discovery," a women's philanthropy organization, in January 2002 to inspire women to become philanthropy leaders by supporting the university's innovative projects and programs.

Ball State's development office provides the group administrative support, works with campus entities on proposals and is responsible for member recruitment, says Mary Ann Olinger, senior director of development.

"Discovery has been a great way to get women involved in philanthropy," Olinger says. "It has provided us an opportunity to get these women better acquainted with the university's strategic plan and the fundraising opportunities available on campus."

Discovery currently has 64 members, each of whom makes an annual contribution of $1,000 for at least three years.

Each year, the group takes proposals from Ball State colleges and departments. An eight-person awards committee reviews proposals to make sure they fit award criteria. Those whose proposals fit the criteria are invited to make oral presentations to the group. The committee then selects proposals that best fit the award criteria. The remaining proposals are placed on a ballot and voted on by all Discovery members.

In 2007, the organization awarded three grants. A typical grant is $15,000 to $25,000, Olinger says. Since 2003, the group has awarded $440,000 to 17 programs.

Olinger says one attraction for membership is that there are few meetings. In addition to being invited to the presentation of oral proposals, members are invited to an annual meeting that includes a luncheon and presentations of projects that received awards from the group that year. A speaker addresses aspects of financial planning.

The university president also invites members to an annual luncheon at her home.

Participation in the meetings is not mandatory and some donors simply send in their check each year, says Olinger, who notes most members live in Indianapolis or Muncie.

Membership in Discovery has not hindered these women's interest in giving other gifts to the university, says Olinger: "That was one of the fears of the development department when Discovery was being proposed, but I can't find one instance where an existing donor switched her giving to the collaborative fund."

Olinger says they have had the most success in recruiting members by meeting with small groups face to face. Prospective members are identified mainly through current members. The group is also promoted on the university's website and through a membership brochure.

Source: Mary Ann Olinger, Senior Director of Development, Ball State University, Muncie, IN. Phone (764) 285-7054. E-mail: molinger@bsu.edu

Gift Club Idea

- To help build a habit of giving among first-time donors, consider establishing a gift club that requires three or more consecutive years of giving. "Membership in The Emerald Club is open to anyone who makes an annual contribution for three or more consecutive years."

71 Ideas for Evaluating Your Gift Clubs, Making Them More Inviting

38 **Annual Giving Societies Attract $1,000-plus Donors**

Give donors the opportunity to support your cause in ways that let them network, socialize and have fun, and you'll greatly increase the likelihood they will continue supporting you for the long run.

Children's Healthcare of Atlanta (Atlanta, GA), for example, has two annual leadership giving societies for $1,000-plus donors: Hope's Circle for female donors and Will's Club for male donors.

Hope's Circle, started five years ago, has nearly 250 members. Will's Club, started about a year ago with about 25 donors, has nearly tripled in size to almost 70 members.

Both are opt-in, meaning members are not automatically enrolled, but must agree to join, says Elesha Mavrommatis, development officer. "The opt-in feature helps us identify donors who want to be contacted on a regular basis," she says. "In effect, they self-identify as being open to a call from a development officer."

Hope's Circle members receive a monthly e-newsletter as well as invitations to behind-the-scenes tours, roundtable discussions with physicians, luncheons and other donor events. Will's Club members receive a quarterly e-newsletter and invitations to member-hosted events. Both groups are recognized in the organization's community report, on signage at the hospitals, and on the medical facility's website.

"While Hope's Circle is staff-driven — I coordinate tours and events — Will's Club is member-driven," says Mavrommatis. "Will's Club members plan their own events and are more active recruiters for the group. For the men, it's a way to socialize with other men who want to support the hospital. I believe that long-term, the men's group will be successful because they feel ownership of it."

Events organized by the men's group to date include skeet shooting, a wine tasting, and a tour and tasting at a local brewery.

Mavrommatis says switching giving society membership due dates from anniversary date to calendar year has made tracking membership much easier. For example, members who give in 2009 are recognized as 2009 donors and have all of 2010 to make a qualifying gift for the next fiscal year.

The giving societies are promoted in the organization's annual fund brochure and on its website, and information about the groups is communicated to major gift officers and corporate gift officers who might have donors who would qualify as members but who may not make a gift directly through the annual fund.

When a qualifying gift comes in through the annual fund, staff send an acknowledgement that includes the opportunity to join the giving society and how to do so.

"When we call them to thank them for their gift, we will also mention it again," she says. "Once they join Hope's Circle, we call to welcome them and send them the last e-newsletter that went out, which includes my contact information sent under my e-mail address. This helps me develop a relationship with these donors."

Will's Club communicates almost exclusively through e-mail.

At Thanksgiving, Mavrommatis sends handwritten cards to all Hope's Circle members. The same happens for Will's Club members. Hope's Circle and Will's Club members also receive a holiday card by e-mail, activities that she says help develop a relationship with these donors, which is an important element in the success of the giving societies.

Source: Elesha Mavrommatis, Development Officer, Children's Healthcare of Atlanta, Atlanta, GA. Phone (404) 785-7336. E-mail: Elesha.Mavrommatis@choa.org

Be sure your gift clubs provide plenty of networking opportunities for your donors and members.

Stay On Top of Gift Club Progress

Whatever you call your top annual gift club (e.g. President's Club, President's Circle, Leadership Society), it's important to keep both staff and key volunteers apprised of its progress on a regular basis. Whether your top gift level starts at $500, $1,000 or more, monthly updates will help encourage everyone to remain on task in meeting goals.

Reports such as the example shown here are particularly helpful if you have a committee or advisory group made up of volunteers expected to identify and solicit likely prospects throughout the year.

President's Circle Progress
(Annual Gifts of $1,000 or more)

	Dollars Raised	Dollar Goal	Donors to Date	Donor Goal
$25,000 +	$0	$50,000	0	2
$10,000 – 24,999	26,000	40,000	2	3
$5,000 – 9,999	24,000	75,000	4	10
$2,500 – 4,999	30,000	60,000	12	20
$1,000 – 2,499	$27,000	40,000	27	40
Total	$107,000	265,000	45	75

Spell Out Qualifications of Planned Giving Society

The 1754 Society of Columbia University (New York, NY) recognizes alumni and friends of Columbia who have made plans for the university through trust, estate or other future gifts.

Promotional materials list the qualifications for membership.

Persons are welcomed into the 1754 Society if they have met one or more of these qualifications:

- Included Columbia in their estate plans through a will or living trust.

- Created a charitable remainder trust, administered by either Columbia or another trustee, which names Columbia as the remainder beneficiary.

- Entered into a charitable-gift annuity agreement with Columbia or invested in one of Columbia's pooled income funds.

- Named Columbia University beneficiary of a life insurance policy or retirement plan.

"Spelling out the types of planned gifts that qualify a donor for membership in our 1754 Society helps them to remember that they have named us a beneficiary of their retirement plan, life insurance policy, life income gift or even their will," says Shawn Mroz, associate director of gift planning. "The society gives donors a welcome reason to self-identify and lets us know of their plans so that we can properly steward them."

Not everyone knows the definition of a planned gift, and other organizations may use similar terms in different ways when describing some of these gifts, says Mroz. "It's easier to define them for people so that the qualifications for membership are clear."

Source: Shawn Mroz, Associate Director of Gift Planning, University Development and Alumni Relations, Office of the Vice President for University Advancement, Columbia University, New York, NY. Phone (212) 870-2473. E-mail: stm2113@columbia.edu

Some planned gift societies include fairly detailed qualifications, including the type of planned gifts that qualify donors for inclusion.

71 Ideas for Evaluating Your Gift Clubs, Making Them More Inviting

41 First Cry Club Makes the Most of Links to Hospital

Rather than trying to create a relationship with a prospect where none existed before, most nonprofits are always on the lookout for links they already have with individuals. The greater the connection, the better the odds of financial support.

Are you looking for established connections with members of your community or region as a way to increase support? You may be surprised at the number of ties that already exist which have yet to be tapped.

Take the hospital that overlooked the number of babies born within its walls over several decades. When officials realized the potential that existed, they began to search old records and discovered over 1,000 names of individuals who had been born there. They created the First Cry Club for anyone who had been born at that hospital and were able to convert some 25 percent of the group into first-time contributors through special marketing efforts.

You may even examine existing giving clubs and expand on them (e.g., Grandparents of Newborns Club).

When considering new clubs and affinity groups, first consider those connections that already exist.

42 Four Ways to Move Donors to the Next Giving Level

As important as it is to retain existing donors year to year, it's equally important to have strategies in place that upgrade past donors to the next levels of annual giving. Increased gifts from past donors can mean the difference between falling short of or surpassing your annual fund goal.

These principles will help you in the upgrading process:

1. **Clearly distinguish benefits at each donor level.** Publicize benefits associated with each of your organization's gift clubs or levels. Clearly distinguish benefits of each level to entice people to move up to the next level.

2. **Involve higher-end donors in upgrading those at lower levels.** Use donor peer pressure to convince others to join. Host prospective member receptions asking higher-level donors to invite lower-level donors.

3. **Make it easy (and painless) to increase one's gift.** Use credit cards, electronic funds transfers from donors' checking accounts, monthly envelopes and other methods to make increased giving as seamless and simple as possible.

4. **Allow donors to decide how their gifts will be used.** Invite existing donors to make a second annual gift — one that moves them to the next giving level — directed to a special project of their choosing. It's more appealing to contribute at higher levels when one has some say in how the gift will be used.

As donors increase their annual giving over time, they will be more prepared and likely to contribute even more significant gifts in the future.

Test Gift Club Appeals

Try segmenting your prospect list by gift clubs. Then send an appeal targeting those within each gift club in an attempt to get them to increase their giving.

Take this approach a step further by sending out four different versions of your letter to a single gift club to test which letter pulls the best response from this particular group of givers.

Grandparents Can Be Formidable Resources

Grandparents can be a forgotten sector in fundraising, especially when the organization is one that doesn't appear to have direct benefits to them. By identifying benefits and creating connections to them, your organization can offer opportunities specifically for these important members of our society.

Children's Medical Foundation of Central Texas' Grandparents Club Stats	
Started in:	2005
Founding members:	39
Charter members:	218
Current prospects:	651
Annual renewal rate:	63%
Annual membership:	$100 minimum
Amount raised in charter year:	$103,175

Mandy Cloud, development officer, Children's Medical Center Foundation of Central Texas (Austin, TX), says their foundation has found great success in a Grandparents Club.

"Our Grandparents Club introduced us to a whole segment of the community who didn't currently have any attachment to the Children's Hospital," Cloud says. "It was very successful from the get-go, because of how we started it."

To start the club, development staff invited a founding committee of 39 grandparents to become members, starting at $100 annual gifts, and also recommending other grandparents for invitation to join the club. In the club's three-year history, prospects gleaned from the founding committee total 651. The club also saw a 63 percent renewal rate between its first and second year and raised $103,175 in its first year.

Cloud points out these keys to the club's success:

• Assuring members they would not be doing any fundraising, that they would be supporting the foundation with their own membership and facilitating introductions to potential members.

• Keeping the tone of the club strictly educational and fun.

In return for their involvement, members are recognized in the foundation's magazine and website, listed on letterhead, receive a monthly e-newsletter and were involved with a naming opportunity at the hospital. Members can also participate in two events per year, a grandmother's tea and a fun event they can do with their grandchildren.

Cloud says the staff plans on adding an additional membership level, starting at $1,000. The foundation staff have also started asking members to host tours of the hospital for friends and colleagues, which is expected to provide a boost in membership.

"Most members ask nonmembers (to join them on tours)." says Cloud. "The greatest impact this club has made is on the connections we have."

Source: Mandy Cloud, Development Officer, Children's Medical Center Foundation of Central Texas, Austin, TX. Phone (512) 324-0170. E-mail: mcloud@seton.org

Content not available in this edition

44 Advisory Council Members Serve as Strong Advocates

Thirty people of various ages, professions and interests come together to serve as advocates for the Sidney Kimmel Comprehensive Cancer Center at Johns Hopkins (Baltimore, MD).

"The mission is for the (advisory council) members to be knowledgeable, informed advocates for the cancer center," Ellen Stifler, director of development, says of the 9-year-old advisory council.

Members of the elite group advocate for the organization. Some refer friends to the cancer center for care. Others share their knowledge of cancer and the center with colleagues and government officials, spearhead fundraising efforts or assist with donor cultivation and gift solicitation.

"There have been times when a particular council member has come with the director or me on a call, and therefore been an advocate for the mission of the cancer center and for the purpose of the ask," Stifler says. "That also lends a real credibility as peer to peer."

While the advisory council benefits the cancer center, Stifler says, membership on the council is mutually rewarding, as it is also a great way to steward current donors.

"It is wonderful stewardship for people who care about the cancer center's mission," Stifler says. "They learn a lot. It is very educational. Additionally, people like to be connected with the leadership of the Kimmel Cancer Center. It brings them into the family."

To create a successful and productive advisory council, remember, "the most important thing is the people you bring in," she says. "Be very careful in selecting the right people. They should be eager for new ideas, have new ideas and respect the director's plans." Additionally, "be willing to rethink and continually work to improve the council."

> **Motivate Advisory Council Members**
>
> Ellen Stifler, director of development, Sidney Kimmel Comprehensive Cancer Center (Baltimore, MD), says she considers the cancer center's advisory council to be strong.
>
> However, its members recently encountered a challenge, when its well-respected and well-liked director died of cancer.
>
> "Our challenge has been to keep our council members interested and invigorated," Stifler says. "It was our goal to maintain momentum even when we all missed our former director. We added new members, and we are continually working to reinvigorate and improve the meetings and interactions."
>
> For example, the council, which meets biannually, will now rotate meeting locations, such as meeting in the kitchen of the cancer center's new patient and family pavilion and including a private tour.
>
> Stifler also plans to make meetings more interactive rather than show-and-tell. She is planning a four-member panel discussion with experts from the cancer center talking on cancer prevention and control, allowing ample time for questions and conversation.

Source: Ellen Stifler, Director of Development, Sidney Kimmel Comprehensive Cancer Center at Johns Hopkins, Baltimore, MD. Phone (410) 516-4262. E-mail: stifler@jhu.edu

45 Ways to Promote New Gift Clubs

- When introducing a new gift club to your constituents, take the one time opportunity to promote charter memberships: "Become a charter member of this new club and receive the following benefits...." or "Get in on the ground floor by becoming a charter member of this special club!"

- If your organization doesn't have much history with giving clubs, start slow, then expand. Begin with one annual giving club, say at the $1,000-plus level, then add another club after you're sure about which direction you want to go with them.

46 Committee Empowers Donors

Donors are unique in the ways they give and in what motivates them to give. One Iowa foundation has found a way to celebrate the distinct giving trends of one group of donors while reaping the benefits.

For nine years, the Iowa State University (ISU) Foundation (Ames, IA) has invited female donors to serve on its women and philanthropy committee and act as advocates for ISU and philanthropy. Women chosen to serve are interested in philanthropy and empowering women, says Melissa Hanna, executive director of annual and special giving.

The committee hosts an annual women and philanthropy workshop where, through keynote speakers and breakout sessions, women learn about creating and maintaining healthy financial positions.

"The committee definitely brings women to the forefront," Hanna says. "We want to focus more attention on that constituency and make sure their philanthropic needs are met. We want women to feel empowered and know they have a voice in this discussion as well."

The proof of the committee's efforts is in the numbers. According to Hanna:

✓ The foundation experienced a 47 percent increase in total number of women donors since 2000. The number jumped from 72,095 women donors by Dec. 31, 2000 to 105,816 by Dec. 31, 2008.

✓ Since 2003, Iowa State saw a 240 percent increase in total dollars given from women, increasing from $10,844,807 in fiscal year 2003 to $36,824,280 in fiscal year 2008.

✓ The average gift from a woman also increased 184 percent from $597 in FY 2003 to $1,696 in FY 2008.

✓ Through 2008, women have given more than $218 million to ISU.

The women and philanthropy committee comprises 17 women from varying professions, all with an interest in ISU. Members may serve two, two-year terms, with those holding the position of board chair granted an extra term. The committee typically meets five times a school year with the first meeting being a fall retreat.

Source: Melissa Hanna, Executive Director of Annual and Special Giving, Iowa State University Foundation, Ames, IA. Phone (515) 294-0596. E-mail: mhanna@foundation.iastate.edu

---

Gift Club Tips

■ To give each of your gift clubs the attention they deserve, appoint a committee to each club and charge them with the responsibility for recruiting, retaining and recognizing donors at that level.

---

47 Rationale for Establishing a Planned Gifts Society

What's the need for a planned gift society — a club which recognizes those who have established planned gifts?

Here's your answer: More than 75 percent of planned gift donors say the charity treats them no differently since learning of their gift.

It's critical to recognize the generosity of planned gift donors even though your charity may not realize that gift for years to come. Additionally, having a planned gifts society in place often motivates donors to inform you of their plans since they want to become a recognized member of your society or club.

71 Ideas for Evaluating Your Gift Clubs, Making Them More Inviting

48 **Messages Challenge Donors to Up Giving Levels**

Moving current supporters of your organization into higher levels of support is an ongoing challenge. For those occasions when you rely on personalized direct mail as a tool for moving donors to a higher level of giving, it helps to draft three or four ways to do so, and then review those methods to determine which is more compelling to the intended audience. Although you may not need to develop entire letters at this stage, it is useful to compare a handful of key messages that are most crucial to the ask.

While the originality of your organization and the services you provide will be key in articulating the exact message, here are three general illustrations aimed at convincing a donor to increase his/her gift over the previous year's contribution.

To move donors or members to a higher level of support, zero in on what you consider to be the most compelling message(s) to accomplish that aim.

Example No. 1 — To maintain what's been accomplished previously.

[Name], I can't begin to tell you how grateful we are for the [amount of last year's gift] you contributed to [name of organization] this past year. The cumulative support from individuals like you really helped make the following accomplishments possible.... (List several highlights/goals met.)

But [Name], I'm going to ask you to do even more this year because it's going to require that everyone do more just to maintain the level of accomplishment that was realized this past year. Here's why....

Specifically, I would like you to consider a gift of....

Example No. 2 — To unleash the possibilities.

[Name], what you and others were able to do for [name of organization] this past year was phenomenal! Thanks to everyone's generosity, we were able to....

But with individuals like you involved with and supporting our efforts, we're confident there's so much more that can be achieved. Need some examples? Consider these....

I know these are lofty goals, but I'm sure you agree that they're worth the sacrifice. That's why I'm hopeful you will increase your previous year's gift of [amount] by 30 percent. Your gift of [proposed amount] will pave the way for....

Everyone associated with [name of organization] and I are counting on you, [Name]. Please help us get there.

Example No. 3 — It's a win for you and a win for us.

[Name], last year you generously contributed [amount] to assist our efforts. And it really helped make a difference in the following ways.... (List several ways here.)

This year I want to extend a special invitation to join the [next giving club or level] by making a contribution of [amount]. By joining this distinctive group of donors, you will enjoy the following benefits....

In addition to this, your increased gift will help us to (list specific or generalized goal).... And that's a win for you and a win for us!

---

49 Beef Up Your Top Gift Club

It's a known fact among veteran fundraisers: to generate more $50,000-and-above gifts, you have to work at expanding the number of upper-level gifts you receive on an annual basis. If your top gift level or club starts at the $1,000 range, for instance, focus annual solicitation efforts on securing more gifts at this level.

Part of generating more upper-level gifts requires offering benefits that will attract those who can afford to give at this level on an annual basis. That's why it makes sense to regularly review those perks. Come up with more exclusive benefits, particularly those that can distinguish your nonprofit from others. Think outside the box in developing appropriate perks for this special group.

Here are some examples you may wish to consider:

- Offer members-only field trips or tours that connect with your mission.

- Get existing members to host one-of-a-kind receptions at their homes, private clubs or corporate offices throughout the year.

- Whenever you host an event that's open to the public, offer exclusive privileges to these special donors — special seating, valet parking, stand and be recognized — that may encourage nonmembers to join their ranks.

- Offer enriching experiences periodically — wine tasting, lectures, investment seminars and more — that appeal to the majority of those giving at this level.

Regularly review those perks that will attract donors to higher levels of support. What can you offer that's more exclusive to this special group?

50 Evaluate Your Gift Clubs' Effectiveness

Most nonprofits' annual giving efforts offer gift categories or giving clubs that include corresponding donor benefits for each level of giving.

To what degree do you analyze each gift club's effectiveness? How successful is each gift club in attracting gifts? Do the corresponding benefits of each gift club encourage increased giving?

To evaluate the effectiveness of your gift clubs:

1. Calculate the number of donors and percentage of overall giving for each club. Which club appears to consistently draw the greatest number of donors? Which accounts for the most gift revenue each year?

2. Determine which gift clubs are attracting the greatest number of increased gifts — in terms of numbers and dollars — from year to year.

3. Analyze benefits associated with each club. Do they become increasingly exclusive as donors move up the ladder of support? Is there sufficient motivation to give more?

Analyzing gift clubs helps you make better judgments about needed changes. You may decide to change gift ranges for a particular club or benefits associated with a specific gift category. Or you may decide a complete revision of your gift clubs is in order.

Analyze the numbers behind each of your gift clubs to determine changes that may be in order.

71 Ideas for Evaluating Your Gift Clubs, Making Them More Inviting

51 Heritage Circle Giving Society Focuses on $1,000-Plus Donors

Staff with the Wisconsin Historical Foundation (Madison, WI) — the official fundraising and gift-receiving organization for the Wisconsin History Society — are focusing on increasing members of its $1,000-plus-a-year Heritage Circle level.

"We've added benefits for members at this level including invitations to exclusive events and activities, complimentary VIP parking privileges, and special recognition in our Honor Roll of Donors and Members in addition to the regular benefits of society membership," says Jeanne L. Engle, the foundation's director of development.

Between July 1, 2009, (the start of the Wisconsin Historical Foundation's fiscal year) and Jan. 5, 2010, some 64 donors made commitments for unrestricted gifts of $1,000 or more, qualifying them for membership in The Heritage Circle. This was up from 49 such donors during the same time in the previous fiscal, says Martha Truby, associate director of annual giving.

Organizers developed a special package for soliciting prospective members from The Heritage Circle level that includes:

- A letter inviting prospective donors to join The Heritage Circle (to which a development staff member or officer usually adds a handwritten note).

- A Heritage Circle brochure — a tri-fold with a pocket into which a list of Heritage Circle donors and a list of Heritage Circle benefits is inserted.

- A customized reply device.

"As we qualify donors who have been identified with having higher financial capacity, we make a personal appeal for membership in The Heritage Circle," says Engle. These personal appeals may be a letter with a handwritten note, a face-to-face visit or a phone call.

To build awareness for The Heritage Circle, they branded it separately with a special logo embedded with the tag line: Leading the Way.

"We created a separate logo because we wanted to reinforce the message that membership in the Heritage Circle means being part of something special," says Truby. "Our goal is to engage them with small group cultivation events, behind-the-scenes tours and insider information. Savvy investors are passionate about our mission and we want them to understand the impact they have on our organization by offering them opportunities to become engaged in what we do."

One new benefit is allowing members to choose their own complimentary gift, says Truby. They can choose one of four books produced by the Wisconsin Historical Society Press, or one of four prints reproduced from the society's extensive image collection. "This is offered with a coupon that is sent with their Heritage Circle member packet," she says. "Several recipients of the coupon added a thank-you note saying they really appreciated the gift."

A key to their early success in attracting Heritage Circle members has been a commitment by development officers to view annual gifts of equal importance as one-time major gifts, says Truby. "Annual gifts help develop a habit of giving that sometimes one large donation can't do."

Sources: Jeanne L. Engle, Director of Development; Martha Truby, Associate Director of Annual Giving, Wisconsin Historical Foundation, Madison, WI. Phone (608) 264-6580 (Engle) Phone (608) 261-9363 (Truby). E-mail: jeanne.engle@wisconsinhistory.org E-mail: martha.truby@wisconsinhistory.org

Content not available in this edition

52 Gift Ideas to Tell Your Top Donors Thanks

Looking to thank your giving clubs' top donors for their support? Consider:

✓ Commemorative certificates and lapel pins so they can proudly display evidence of their commitment to you.

✓ A plaque or engraved gift presented to major giving club donors by a direct recipient/beneficiary of their gifts.

✓ Gifts donated by community members — magazine subscriptions, coupons, gift certificates — which represent no cost to your organization, but make donors feel like they are getting star treatment.

53 Simple Giving Level Change Boosts Sponsorships

The Institute for Systems Biology (Seattle, WA) experienced an increase in five-figure sponsorships and a jump of nearly $2,000 in the average sponsorship, all thanks to a simple change.

Previously, the institute offered sponsorships at $2,500; $5,000; $10,000; and $15,000 for its two-day annual international scientific symposium. This year, however, the research organization added a fifth level: $25,000.

"By adding the $25,000 level, we not only moved some of our current sponsors, we also saw an increase in five-figure sponsorships," says Amanda Dunkin, manager of the P4 Fund. "Our sponsorship average from 2004-2007 was $8,375. Once we reviewed our sponsorship levels, our sponsorship average went up to $10,355. From 2004-2007, 33 percent of our sponsorships were $15,000 and above. In 2008, 55 percent of our sponsorships were $15,000 and above."

Review sponsorship levels annually, Dunkin says. When doing so, she advises:

1. **Evaluate regular sponsors.** How long have they been sponsors? Have they remained at a consistent sponsorship level? How many sponsors are at the top two levels? "As development professionals, we're always thinking about moving our donors ... but often forget to move our sponsors to the next level," Dunkin says. Before doing so, however, consider the economy. If it's a hard economic year, she says, it doesn't make sense to expect sponsors to still give at their previous levels.

2. **Consider your organization's age.** If sponsorship levels were set in your early years but now you're an established organization, adapt your sponsorship levels accordingly.

3. **Utilize benchmark studies.** "These studies can and should be your best friend," Dunkin says. "Look at local organizations doing the same thing, but also those doing different things that target the same demographic. Also, don't be afraid to look at similar organizations nationally."

Form a Sponsors' Society

You no doubt have gift clubs for donors who contribute at higher levels, but have you considered one that caters strictly to sponsors?

Why not establish some form of sponsors' society that provides appropriate recognition and benefits for those who establish generous sponsorships?

Such a club or society would help encourage repeat sponsorships and also serve to attract new sponsors wanting to be a part of this exclusive group.

The society would also foster greater camaraderie among those who sponsor programs and events at your nonprofit.

Source: Amanda Dunkin, Manager of the P4 Fund, Institute for Systems Biology, Seattle, WA. Phone (206) 732-1444. E-mail: adunkin@systemsbiology.org

71 Ideas for Evaluating Your Gift Clubs, Making Them More Inviting

54 Annual Fund Donors Join Giving Circles

Annual fund donors at The Walters Art Museum (Baltimore, MD) receive more than a thank-you: They become members of the museum's annual giving circles. Donors contributing $250 or more join one of seven annual giving circles, each with unique benefits.

"Making people feel like they are valued and part of the spirit of a program is important," says Julia Keller, manager of individual and corporate giving circles.

To do so, the circles offer donors unique privileges outlined below:

Sustainer ($250 to $749):
- Invitation to one monthly reception and tour with museum leadership.
- Two single-use parking passes.
- Discounts on museum tours and events, as well as children's and family programs.
- Subscription to The Walters Magazine, which features exclusive news about the museum and is published three times a year.
- Reciprocal privileges at 30 select art museums across the United States.
- Discounts at local restaurants.
- A 10-percent savings in the museum's store and cafe.
- Recognition in the annual report.

Patron ($750 to $1,499):
- Sustainer benefits plus an invitation for two to the Patrons' Preview, allowing a private look at one of the museum's special exhibits before it opens to the public.

Curators' Circle ($1,500 to $2,499):
- Patron benefits plus an invitation for two to the Curators' Choice reception. Donors have the opportunity to hear in-depth discussions by the curators of current projects followed by cocktails in the museum's Sculpture Court.
- Donors receive four single-use parking passes.
- Special recognition on the Honor Wall, located in the lobby of the museum.

Directors' Circle ($2,500 to $4,999):
- Curators' Circle benefits plus invitation for two to the Director's Dinner, an annual dinner that gives donors a chance to dine with the museum's international board of directors and hear speakers from nationally recognized museums address current issues.

Henry and William Walters' Circle ($5,000 to $9,999):
- Directors' Circle benefits along with a private lunch and/or consultation with a curator or conservator.
- Invitation to join the Collectors' Circle Seminar Series. The four-part series affords donors the opportunity to attend an in-depth seminar by museum curators and conservators, with seminars presented in the original Walters' family parlor.

Founders' Circle ($10,000 to $24,999):
- Henry and William Walters' Circle benefits plus a private dinner and tour for four with the museum's director.
- Invitation to join the Director's Travel Program and tour cities around the world with the chance to view some of the world's finest art collections.

Benefactor ($25,000 or more):
- Founders' Circle benefits as well as a private dinner and tour for eight with the museum's director.

While several of the benefits were in place when Keller joined the museum staff in August 2005, she says she periodically reviews benefits to keep them current and is always looking for incentives, such as ways to engage donors and give them more personal access to the museum.

Source: Julia Keller, Manager of Individual and Corporate Giving Circles, The Walters Art Museum, Baltimore, MD. Phone (410) 547-9000, ext. 314. E-mail: jkeller@thewalters.org

Pay particular attention to distinguishing the benefits between each of your gift clubs or, in this instance, giving circles.

71 Ideas for Evaluating Your Gift Clubs, Making Them More Inviting

If you really want to make an effort to build your endowment, consider creating a club or society aimed at recognizing those who make endowment gifts.

55 Establish a Society for Endowment Donors

There are clubs for those who make annual gifts at the $1,000-and-above level. There are heritage societies for those who make planned gifts. Why not create a special society for anyone who establishes a named endowment fund?

Giving clubs and societies accomplish two important goals: 1) they recognize donors' generosity; and 2) they motivate people to give — to increase their giving or to make first-time gifts. So it makes perfect sense to establish an esteemed society for this group of high-level contributors.

Here's an outline of how to get an endowment society up and running:

1. Get your board to buy into and back the idea of an endowment society which recognizes all donors who have created named endowment funds.

2. Assemble a committee made up of existing donors who have established named funds. Be sure to have board representation on the committee as well.

3. Draft a committee description and a yearly plan that may include:
   a) How you intend to recognize society members.
   b) How you intend to induct new members into the society.
   c) The benefits of the society's membership.
   d) A yearlong schedule of events for members to attend.
   e) An action plan for identifying, cultivating and soliciting new prospects to establish named endowment funds.

4. Get businesses and/or individuals to underwrite costs associated with this new program (e.g., keepsakes to be presented to members, member receptions, etc.).

Here's an example of a club in which members meet to discuss public television programming.

56 Program Club Boosts Goodwill and Giving

What started as a simple marketing idea has turned into a way to increase revenue and build better relationships with supporters, says Elise Marquam-Jahns, director of planned giving, Twin Cities Public Television, Inc. (St. Paul, MN). The tpt-PBS Program Club is like a book club, with members discussing public television programming rather than the latest bestseller. There are six different Program Clubs — one that meets monthly at the station between June and November and five others that meet at various senior complexes around the Twin Cities between October and June.

People watch the selected show in their own home and then visit one of the six locations to discuss it with other participants. Those who attend the station club also get to hear behind-the-scenes information from a tpt staff person, including producers talking about their latest local or national productions.

Marquam-Jahns says the club tends to draw bright, articulate and involved people who are active in the community. "The feedback has been extremely positive. People enjoy the learning opportunities, the chance to meet others who have similar interests and the chance to make new friends."

The club has also helped tpt increase their revenue. Says Marquam-Jahns, "Many of the individuals who were $25-50 annual supporters have become major donors and/or planned giving donors. Since 2001, 31 Program Club members have become Visionary Society members, including tpt in their will or estate plan."

Marquam-Jahns' best advice for someone looking to start a similar program? "Give it some time to develop. We started with a core group of 8 people. Now we have 50 to 60 who attend the club at the station each month and over 125 attending at the senior centers."

Source: Elise Marquam-Jahns, Director of Planned Giving, Twin Cities Public Television, Inc., St. Paul, MN. Phone (651) 229-1276. E-mail: emjahns@tpt.org.

71 Ideas for Evaluating Your Gift Clubs, Making Them More Inviting

 57 Let Employees Direct How Funds Are Used

Every year, the staff at Saint Patrick Hospital (Missoula, MT) donate more than $100,000 to their hospital's Health Foundation.

Donations come via their 30 Minute Club, a giving program that allows employees to donate 30 minutes worth of pay from each bi-monthly paycheck and direct the money toward hospital programs of their choosing.

Kathryn McCleerey, health foundation annual campaign development officer, says that the 30 Minute Club (nicknamed 30 MC) is a long-standing part of the Spirit of Giving campaign that helps employees support the hospital in ways most meaningful to them.

McCleerey explains how the 30 MC giving program works:

✓ Employees choose the amount they wish to donate per paycheck: either 30 minutes worth of pay or another specified amount.

✓ Employees then select from more than 30 programs to support, from cardiology to cancer, scholarship funds to patient support groups.

✓ Every dollar that the employee sacrifices from his/her paycheck goes directly into the fund that he/she has selected, with nothing taken out for expenses.

Because the giving program deals with an internal group of donors, McCleery says, it is low-cost and low-maintenance. It is a part-time job for a single employee to promote and serve as the program's point person. Promotional activities are low-cost because they can occur during established events, such as new employee orientation and the employee benefits fair.

Additionally, she says, the program is designed to be self-sufficient: Using the hospital website and employee intranet, employees may sign up, change their level of participation, and change the program they wish to support. The foundation then communicates with human resources to let them know the amount to deduct from each paycheck, as the employee has directed, McCleerey says, noting, "Employees appreciate that response time is almost immediate when any change is requested."

McCleerey says more than 30 percent of employees participate in the program. The foundation hosts an annual thank-you luncheon or breakfast for the participants.

Beyond that, she says, the program is its own reward. "[Participants] know that 100 percent of their contribution is being directed to the programs they care most deeply about. Within our gentle culture, we do not directly solicit employees for the program — it is appropriate for us to simply promote and inform."

Source: Kathryn L. McCleerey, Development Officer, St. Patrick Hospital and Health Foundation, Missoula, MT. Phone (406) 327-3052.
E-mail: kmccleerey@saintpatrick.org. Website: www.stpatsfoundation.org

Content not available in this edition

Content not available in this edition

58 Draw More Major Donors With Upper-level Membership Perks

How does an organization ensure that upper-level memberships ($1,000 per year and up) are attractive to individuals of means? By providing at least one of three things, says Lauren Davidson, individual giving manager at the Contemporary Jewish Museum (CJM) of San Francisco, CA: access, recognition or opportunities for socialization.

Museum benefits offering access include priority admission, curator-led tours and invitations to exclusive receptions and artist events. Recognition-based benefits include an annual donor wall, newsletter mention and the option to underwrite major exhibitions and programs.

Benefits providing unique opportunities for socialization often focus on travel opportunities such as a tour of a donor's private glass collection or a tour of featured artists' Bay-area studios.

In offering upper-level benefits, Davidson says, they take into consideration that high-end donors may see the value of benefits differently than persons who give at lesser levels. Davidson takes recognition as an example, noting that the desire for public acknowledgement often wanes at the highest levels of giving.

"People giving $10,000 to one institution are often giving it to several others," she says, "so recognition is not as important to them. We find it generally matters more to those in the $1,000 to $5,000 range because many of them give only to us."

Similarly, Davidson says, when offering social opportunities, museum officials often distinguish between on-site events (generally offered at the $1,000 level) and off-site events (offered at $1,800 and up). Doing so, she says, provides a gradation of benefits that encourages individuals to upgrade memberships.

Regarding value benefits such as guest passes and gift shop discounts, she says that when it comes to upper-level donors, "these are not hugely compelling, but they're not meaningless, either," noting that members at the $1,000-plus levels do make use of discounts and special sales.

The most important step to determining benefits that both reward members and encourage them to move up giving levels, she says, is understanding members' fundamental motivation. "We find about 75 percent of higher-level donors are mission-based, rather than benefits-based. The key, then, is structuring benefits to make sure those individuals feel involved with the institution they believe in. It all comes back to building and strengthening relationships."

Strategy Moves Major Donors To Higher Giving Levels

To move individuals to higher (and more profitable) levels of membership, officials at the Contemporary Jewish Museum (San Francisco, CA) rely on a 12-member development committee.

Comprising upper-level members and trustees, this committee offers a range of suggestions on events and benefits and also reviews renewing memberships monthly to decide whom to ask to move to a higher level of membership, says Lauren Davidson, individual giving manager.

Because museum officials have found not asking to be one of the biggest obstacles to development, the majority of members are generally invited to upgrade. Staff at the museum's development office offers background research and coaching if needed, but it is almost always committee members who make the ask.

"These are some pretty savvy fundraisers, and peer-to-peer solicitation has been a very effective tool for us," says Davidson, adding that around a quarter of donors increased their gifts by an average of 80 percent in 2009.

Source: Lauren Davidson, Individual Giving Manager, Contemporary Jewish Museum, San Francisco, CA. Phone (415) 655-7829. E-mail: Ldavidson@thecjm.org

71 Ideas for Evaluating Your Gift Clubs, Making Them More Inviting

59 Junior Associates Circle Targets Under-40 Members

Nonprofits depend on cultivating successive generations of leadership. This is precisely what staff at the Dallas Museum of Art (Dallas, TX) do with their Junior Associates Circle, says Kimberly Bryan, director of donor circle membership.

"Members who support the museum in their 20s and 30s are far more likely to become major donors and trustees as they mature and their resources grow," Bryan says. "It's a way to plan for the future."

The Junior Associates Circle aims to ease younger persons into higher levels of support, she says. Restricted to persons under 40 years of age, membership offers many of the benefits of a full $2,000 Associate membership for just $625.

The under-40 level also offers benefits tailored to younger audiences such as special educational opportunities, tours, exhibitions and travel events. The programming schedule features monthly events culminating in the annual Juniors-only black-tie fundraiser, An Affair of the Art.

Now in its 19th year, the Junior Associates Circle is one of the museum's more active groups, says Bryan, with about 400 household memberships — roughly equal to that of the Associates Circle itself.

Targeting younger supporters is not without its challenges, says Bryan. For instance, the demographic is often highly transient, and relationships can easily be lost when supporters relocate in pursuit of careers, marriage or other opportunities.

Outweighing the challenges are the benefits of engaging people at a young age. "For many people, the circle begins an association that can last for decades or sometimes a lifetime," Bryan says.

For organizations looking to target younger demographics, Bryan recommends strong volunteer leadership. "Peer-to-peer interaction," she says, "is definitely the best way to get a younger group going and keep it strong."

Source: Kimberly Camuel Bryan, Director of Donor Circle Membership, Dallas Museum of Art, Dallas, TX. Phone (214) 922-1242. E-mail: kbryan@DallasMuseumofArt.org

Here's an example of a club that targets the under-40 crowd.

60 What It Takes to Get a Gift Club Up and Running

When development staff at William Jewell College decided to replace their existing leadership giving society with one that focused on a donor's long-term commitment to leadership gifts, they knew they had their work cut out for them.

Here's a look at their efforts to make the new club successful, by the numbers, six months into the process:

- Sent a select group of 700 people personal invitations from the college president.
- Had personal contact with over 300 recipients of the invitation.
- Sent first issue of the quarterly newsletter that focused on affirming how members' annual investments are benefiting the college.
- Twenty member-households have given at the leadership level this year, but have not yet made the commitment for long-term giving.
- Ten individuals have given at the leadership level this year, but have declined membership because they could not commit to long-term giving.
- Confirmed 100 new member-households to date, more than half way to their first-year goal of 150.

Source: Andrea Meloan, Director of the Jewell Fund, William Jewell College, Liberty, MO. Phone (816) 415-7831. E-mail: meloana@william.jewell.edu.

Do you have a gift club or society that encourages and rewards long-term giving?

Be sure your gift clubs fully communicate the impact that gifts are having on your organization and those you serve.

61 Make Your Giving Societies Distinctive

Giving societies are a time-honored method of specialty stewardship — a great way to honor top donors by making them feel special. In a down economy, when major gifts are difficult to come by, it is even more important to make your giving societies stand out.

But how? Comparatively, the most successful fundraising organizations share this piece of advice above all — donors who commit to certain levels of giving want to know that their contribution is making a difference. Your giving society should:

1. Grant the donor exclusive access to information and events within the organization.

2. Connect the donor to the change he/she is affecting within your organization on a personal level.

3. Work on three levels: to attract new donors, to steward donors who already have a connection to your organization, and to attract existing donors to give at higher levels.

To achieve the three key goals, listed above, your giving society should:

❑ **Host events specifically to recognize advancements made via donations.** For instance, host a scholarship ceremony that pairs each scholarship recipient with a giving club member the recipient can mention in his/her speech and thank in person, allowing giving club members to literally put a face with their gift.

❑ **Send editorial clippings about advancements at your organization.**

❑ **Provide tours of your facility where giving club members can see their generosity at work.** The more they give, the more VIP treatment they receive. Lower-level donors might go on a group tour while higher-level donors go on individual tours with high-ranking members of your organization's leadership.

❑ **Feature donors in media presentations about your organization.**

❑ **Get creative with the breakdown of your giving club levels.** Focus less on the dollar amount and more on the giving club's community. For instance:

• A Heritage Society can recognize individuals who remember your organization in wills or insurance policies.

• An Emerging Donors giving club can honor younger donors.

• A Lifetime Club encourages long-term, sustained giving.

❑ **Personalize.** Even in a big institution, each member of a giving club needs to feel exclusive and special. To achieve this:

• Write correspondence by hand, whenever reasonable.

• Supplement business calls with personal touches; for instance call on the donor's anniversary of membership.

• Give out color-coded tickets to events. You know that not everyone can be invited to all events, but the donor receiving the events package will get the feeling of being part of something elite.

Sources: Marie J. Maher, Director of Development and Alumni Relations, University of Minnesota, Rochester, MN. Phone (507) 258-8059. E-mail: mmaher@umn.edu
Keri Muuss, Director of Communication and Donor Relations, The Children's Hospital Foundation, Aurora, CO. E-mail: kmuuss@tchfden.org. Phone (720) 777-1765.
Website: www.thechildrenshospitalfoundation.org

71 Ideas for Evaluating Your Gift Clubs, Making Them More Inviting

62 Five Ways to Promote New Gift Societies

Marketing was critical to getting the word out when they created their new leadership giving society Andrea Meloan, director of the Jewell Fund, William Jewell College (Liberty, MO), says. "We not only had to market to alumni and potential members," Meloan says, "we also had to educate past giving society members on what the new society is and how it differed from our former program."

Meloan's staff continues using the following strategies to ensure their constituents know about the new John Priest Greene Society:

1. Completing personal follow-up with recipients of the invitation to join the society, including meetings, e-mails and phone calls. The student call center also contacts those who don't respond by a given date.

2. Holding one-on-one meetings to provide information about the college today, share its hopes for the future and ask for a wide variety of feedback, including individuals' charitable priorities and knowledge of giving programs like the new society.

3. Creating and distributing a quarterly newsletter from the college's president that provides small chunks of campus news that is unique to any other communication they distribute and is easy to read.

4. Visiting members in person when possible.

5. Promoting the society with feature stories and full-page promotional pieces in the college's various publications.

Meloan says it's important not to stop at mass-marketing measures. "Reach out and follow-up to talk about the new giving society in one-on-one and small group settings as often as possible. This cements the importance of the giving society and encourages feedback about your organization and the future likelihood of individuals to join the new society."

Source: Andrea Meloan, Director of the Jewell Fund, William Jewell College, Liberty, MO. Phone (816) 415-7831. E-mail: meloana@william.jewell.edu.

Think outside the box about the ways in which you publicize your gift clubs and make nondonors aware of giving opportunities and accompanying benefits.

63 Encourage Society Members With Creative Gestures

Q. What incentives do you offer to motivate your donors?

"We recently started offering a drawing for a monthly prize to encourage our Society of Founders members to give early in the year. Every June there is always a big rush of last-minute gifts right before our fiscal year deadline. We wanted to encourage our donors to give early, and we wanted to do that in a way that would add to their experience as members of the Society of Founders.

"As soon as someone makes a gift at the Founders' level ($1,500-plus for all but recent graduates), or starts monthly payments on that level, they are eligible for the drawing from that month to the end of the fiscal year.

"We have received many positive responses about the new program, along with e-mails from people asking if they are eligible or what they can do to become eligible."

— *Mandalyn Thompson, Assistant Director of Annual Giving, Hampden-Sydney College, Hampden-Sydney, VA*

Match Giving Incentives To Your Constituency

Thinking about implementing a gift incentive program for donors? First, evaluate your constituency to learn what your supporters might find valuable or exciting.

Mandalyn Thompson, assistant director of annual giving, Hampden-Sydney College (Hampden-Sydney, VA) says they didn't want to simply give away hats or T-shirts because they wanted the prize items to be of considerable worth to those eligible for the drawing. They have included items such as college-logo cufflinks and dinner with the college's president in their drawings for the Society of Founders monthly drawing.

64 Monogram Club Marks Connection Between Former and Current Athletes

The University of Notre Dame (Notre Dame, IN) prides itself on having an active alumni base and, says Communications Associate Mark LaFrance, "athletics is a huge part of that." With 7,000 members, their Monogram Club is proof positive of that. Centered on both the past and future of the school's athletics, it's clear that the club is a success.

One of the biggest reasons for that is a hugely active and successful board. "They hold prominent places in their communities," says LaFrance, "and they know how Notre Dame helped them get where they are." As a result they are committed to making the club a success. "From a membership advocacy perspective their contributions are significant. If you don't have the people to make (your recruitment efforts) shine, your efforts can be pretty futile."

Funds raised through membership dues, individual contributions and raffles and auctions are used to support initiatives such as sponsoring team travel to international training, granting scholarships for community service, purchasing championship and post-season gifts for student-athletes and purchasing laptops so student-athletes can study on the road, among other things.

Benefits to members include advanced access to football tickets and access to golf courses on campus. Current student-athletes can also be paired with successful alumni in a field and geographic area where they are interested in working. The club helps plan sports reunions, recognizes former athletes at half-time of games, offers pre-football game buffets and post-game Masses and holds a semi-annual letter jacket ceremony with gifts for multi-letter students. Most significantly, the club offers the BBR Scholarship Fund, which allows the children of former student-athletes to receive scholarships to attend Notre Dame.

Says LaFrance, "The Monogram Club promotes the legacy of Notre Dame Athletics. Every student athlete that has lettered at Notre Dame is a part of the society. It connects former and current student athletes to bridge the gap."

Source: Mark LaFrance, Communications Associate, Monogram Club, University of Notre Dame, Notre Dame, IN. Phone (574) 631-8476. E-mail: Mark.LaFrance.3@nd.edu.

Make a point to engage your board in gift and member club decisions.

65 Exercise for Increasing $1,000-plus Contributors

What role does a gift club or gift level play in motivating people to give to your organization? And when was the last time you evaluated your gift clubs to be sure they are accomplishing their intended purposes?

To get annual contributors to move up to your $1,000-and-above level, go to some of those donors in your next level down, perhaps donors at the $500 to $999 level. Set up a series of small group focus sessions with those at this level, say seven or eight to a group. Meet with each group and explain that you are attempting to make giving at the $1,000-and-above level a more meaningful and rewarding experience for those who give at that level. Point out the benefits of giving at that level, and offer some background regarding the makeup of that group. Then ask for those present to share their perceptions about that gift level — what appeals to them, what they are indifferent about and what they would change.

Although it may appear obvious that part of your rationale in bringing them together is to upgrade them to that higher level of annual giving, it should also be apparent that you have a legitimate reason for seeking their perceptions. Their input may, in fact, lead you to make some changes with your $1,000-plus giving club.

To encourage annual donors to upgrade their giving, ask them what it would take to make that happen.

71 Ideas for Evaluating Your Gift Clubs, Making Them More Inviting

66. Pooling Major Donors' Gifts Adds Up For Giving Group, Hospital Foundation

St. Joseph's Hospital Foundation (Tampa, FL) is reaching out to philanthropic women through a new group called Philanthropic Women of St. Joseph's. The leadership network of community-minded women has a mission of changing and saving lives in the Tampa Bay community by investing in collaboration with other women leaders.

Members pool their annual philanthropic contributions and decide together which St. Joseph's Hospital project to fund each year.

Nora Gunn, the foundation's director of development, says they have two strategic objectives for the group:

1. To build the capacity of their fundraising program by increasing the number of $1,000 gifts.

2. To make a concentrated effort to engage women at this level who are interested in pooling their gifts.

The group's two founders hand-selected a steering committee, whose members were asked to recruit their friends. "It spread like wildfire," says Gunn. "Women were attracted by the ability to pool their gifts to increase the impact of their $1,000 gift. They also liked the idea of sharing experiences and health education with like-minded, entrepreneurial women."

The group offers three membership levels:

- **Founder:** A $25,000 commitment paid over one to five years. Founder members receive permanent recognition as Philanthropic Women of St. Joseph's and are permanent members of the steering committee.

- **Leader:** A $10,000 commitment paid over one to five years. Members receive recognition as Philanthropic Women Leaders for the length of their pledge and may serve a two-year term as a steering vommittee member.

- **Member:** A $1,000 annual commitment.

Membership currently includes two at the founder level, nine at the leader level and 55 at the member level, Gunn says.

Each year, the membership is presented with three possible projects to fund. The three projects are based on the hospital's funding priorities. The steering committee researches each project, presents them to the entire group and the group votes on which project to fund.

Members are encouraged to attend three scheduled meetings per year: a speaker's luncheon, which serves as the group's membership drive; a project selection meeting in which the group votes on which project to fund; and a celebration that includes a presentation by those who were impacted by the gift. The latter two meetings are held in a member's home.

"The group has appreciated the fact that they can be as involved as they would like," says Gunn. "For those looking to build a strong allegiance to their nonprofit, this is absolutely the right structure. We have made many friends we otherwise wouldn't have known had an interest in our organization. It's also a great way to build a donor base for future major gifts."

Source: Nora Gunn, Director of Development, St. Joseph's Hospital Foundation, Tampa, FL. Phone (813) 872-0979. E-mail: nora.gunn@baycare.org

Some gift clubs are gender-specific in their fundraising and recognition approach.

Legends Society Recognizes $1 Million Donors

Colby-Sawyer College (New London, NH) recognizes its $1 million-plus donors with membership in the Legends Society at an induction dinner program and through the installation of a specially designed and written, etched brass plaque for the college's recognition wall.

Early in 2003, Colby-Sawyer established the Legends Society to honor individuals and families whose lifetime giving to the college reached $1 million and above. "The gifts of these special benefactors provided support to enhance the quality of our academic programs, optimized the setting for learning, and provided endowment to build the financial strength of the college," says Sharon Ames, manager of public programs and stewardship. "The Legends Society was created to recognize and salute their extraordinary philanthropy."

At the inaugural event in the fall that year, the first members were inducted into the society with a recognition dinner program. Some of the new members were deceased, but most were living Legends and many were couples, she says.

"Following dinner, the college's president spoke in celebration of this gathering of Colby-Sawyer's most generous benefactors and of the impact these exemplary gifts provide for our institution," says Ames. During the program, the chair of the Board of Trustees and a select group of board members, serving as presenters, offered special remarks and recognized each of the new Legends. The Legends Society wall was unveiled at the inaugural event and was a focal point for celebratory photos with the president and/or family members.

Subsequent induction events have been held as additional members became eligible, says Ames. The events still feature a recognition dinner program, but instead of traveling to the Legends Society wall, the presenter now simply reads the plaque text as part of his or her new Legends presentation. Special care is taken to customize the event to the wishes of the new Legends member, she says. "Their families and select friends are included on the invitation list and the overall size of the gathering is consistent with their comfort level." Full Legends members as well as prospective Legends and current trustees are also invited. There are currently 44 Legends Society members.

Ames says the success of the program is based on the quality and personalization of the Legends recognition program, the outstanding individual attention given to each of the society members, and the valuable current campus communication offered to these high-level donors. "Our Legends share a deep and genuine desire to join their peers in helping to make a transformative difference on our campus," she says. "A multi-million dollar donor couple, who had no prior connection to the college, was impressed and decided to make Colby-Sawyer a philanthropic priority after hearing one of our first Legends speak of his sense of fulfillment over the significant changes his gift made possible for our college."

Source: Sharon Ames, Manager of Public Programs and Stewardship, Colby-Sawyer College, New London, NH.
Phone (603) 526-3720.
E-mail: sames@colby-sawyer.edu

Content not available in this edition

Content not available in this edition

Gift Clubs & Societies

71 Ideas for Evaluating Your Gift Clubs, Making Them More Inviting

68 Create a Program That Cultivates, Honors Women

The University of Arkansas' Women's Giving Circle (Fayetteville, AR) was created in 2002 by the founding members of the university's Women and Philanthropy Committee of the Campaign for the Twenty-First Century as a way to transform women's giving to the university and increase their awareness of their power as philanthropists.

"They were compelled to create something that would live past the end of the capital campaign," says Susan Neyman, director of annual programs.

The group's 85 members, made up of alumnae and friends of the university, pool their $1,000 annual cash gifts and vote on which projects within the university to support each year. Faculty and staff members and their spouses, and current students and recent graduates of the university can join the giving circle for a $500 annual gift. The Women's Giving Circle has so far given almost $300,000 to 20 university projects that have some impact on women's lives.

"The giving circle allows women to give the way they would like to give," says Neyman. "By combining their gifts, they can be involved in making an $80,000 annual gift rather than a single $1,000 gift."

Together, giving circle members choose how to direct the group's pooled resources through an annual grants award process. A committee reviews proposals submitted by various university departments and then sends them out to the membership, which narrows the proposals down to around seven projects. The director of those projects makes a presentation to the group, and then the members rank each project and vote individually. After a final discussion of which projects should be funded, the awards are made.

The university also periodically provides programs to educate giving circle members about philanthropy in a symposium format. Speakers who have a message about their personal philanthropy have included ABC'S Robin Roberts, Mary Lou Retton and Linda Bloodworth-Thomason. The symposium is used as a forum for publicly presenting awards in a big check format as well as a recruitment event.

The keys to the success of the program, says Neyman, are that it is volunteer-driven and led by a committee that helps women understand they have a significant amount of philanthropic power.

Source: Susan Neyman, Director of Annual Giving, University of Arkansas, Fayetteville, AR. Phone (479) 575-3238. E-mail: sneyman@uark.edu

Do you have a particular group of would-be donors who deserve more attention? Establish a club or society that's exclusive to that group.

69 Giving Society Members Receive Unique Piece of History

With Alumna Elzelien Hartog's $100,000 gift to Knox College's (Galesburg, IL) Center for Global Studies to create the Joseph J. Hartog Endowment for Global Studies and Scholarship, she became a member of the College's Lincoln-Douglas Society. The Society honors donors with cumulative lifetime giving of $100,000 or more. These donors are honored at a public event and presented with a unique keepsake representing the college's history — bookends representing Abraham Lincoln and Stephen A. Douglas. Knox College is the only remaining site of the famous Lincoln-Douglas debates of 1858. The bookends were designed and sculpted by an alumna whose interest in art was kindled by a Knox professor.

Members of the Lincoln-Douglas Society also receive an annual book mailing from Knox featuring a book written by a faculty member that would have wide appeal among the members in the Society.

Source: Beverly Holmes, Vice President for Advancement, Knox College, Galesburg, IL. Phone (309) 341-7755. E-mail: bholmes@knox.edu

Some gift societies recognize a donor's cumulative lifetime giving.

Major donors deserve a much more engaging level of attention to recognize their generosity and maintain their commitment.

70   **Major Donor Club Helps Raise Major Gifts**

The University of Tennessee (UT) (Knoxville, TN) Development Council is made up of approximately 70 major donors who have contributed more than $100,000 individually to a UT department or unit.

"Development Council members are interested in being more engaged with the university and want to interact with administration at the presidential and board of trustee level," says Suzy Garner, director of development. "They are generous, passionate about UT (specifically those areas which they support), and want to be advocates."

Each Development Council member makes an annual gift of $1,000 to fund the Council's meeting activities and the annual Development Council Awards Dinner, held each fall, where UT's highest awards are presented, including the Development Council Service Award, the Philanthropist(s) of the Year Award, and the Haslam Presidential Medal. The group meets formally twice a year, in spring and fall. In between meetings, they participate in various activities, says Garner, including:

- Touring campus facilities made possible with private donations.
- Interacting with faculty and students.
- Attending athletic events.
- Assisting with solicitations of other alumni or friends.
- Assisting with corporate relations.
- Talking with their state representatives who direct funds to UT.
- Hosting regional campaign events or assisting in the organization of corporate events.
- Serving as campaign leaders for specific departmental units.
- Making introductions and recommendations regarding other potential prospects.
- Working directly with specific development officers.

New members are recruited through current members who make recommendations, and development staff is asked to make formal nominations, she says. Most members live in Tennessee since that is where the university's highest concentration of donors are located, but they encourage participation from across the country. Their current chair lives in California.

The selection of a chair is informal, says Garner, and he or she typically has served as a vice chair, has experience serving on the executive committee, and is interested in continuing his or her service. The vice chairs are selected based on their involvement with the council and UT, meeting attendance, and their interest in serving, she says: "We ask for input from development staff, the President, and the current chair when selecting vice chairs. The current chair's input is highly valued, and he or she ultimately extends the invitation to the new vice chair."

To keep members engaged and participating in the Council, Garner says, they work hard to respond to members' feedback — whether that is making changes to meeting schedules or program content: "Many of our members go on to serve UT in other ways, such as on the UT Foundation Board and even on the Board of Trustees. We want them to feel like insiders and encourage as much presidential and trustee interaction as possible. Also, we try not to take up so much of their time that they can't continue to help those areas at UT about which they are most passionate."

They are in the process of fine tuning their membership expectations and developing a self-assessment tool for members, she says.

Source: Suzy Garner, Director of Development, The University of Tennessee, Knoxville, TN. Phone (865) 974-2115. E-mail: suzy.garner@tennessee.edu

71 Ideas for Evaluating Your Gift Clubs, Making Them More Inviting

71 Make Time to Evaluate Membership Categories

    Tiered membership categories help identify top fundraising and leadership prospects but need to be reviewed periodically, says Dana Hines, president and CEO, Membership Consultants (St. Louis, MO).

    Here, Hines discusses keys to building an effective membership strategy.

How often should organizations review a membership structure?

"To simply keep up with inflation, we recommend adjusting dues every three years. This reflects the economic environment and avoids the kind of drastic rate increases that alienate members."

What should go into a review of membership categories?

"We advise a cost-benefit analysis of all categories and benefits, with particular attention given to the perceived value of benefits versus the costs to actually deliver them.

    "Our rule of thumb is that any membership should yield around 50 percent profit. In a $100 membership, for example, the cost of all benefits and the costs of servicing that membership should total no more than around $50."

How many membership levels should there be? And how large?

"Categories should roughly double at every level: $75, $100, $250, $500, $1,000 is a common progression. We also recommend listing all levels on every piece of literature. Some organizations think that only lower categories should be included, but first-time members do join at upper levels, and you don't want to needlessly squander that support."

Are any membership problems especially common?

"Many organizations, particularly those with membership programs built by a board of directors or advisory committee, have far too many membership categories. Streamlining can be difficult, but if people face too many options, they sometimes don't act at all. Better in the long run to lump some things together and create a system that is approachable and understandable."

What should organizations watch out for when restructuring membership categories or benefits?

"Steer away from any benefits that could create ill will. Parking privileges are a favorite benefit of visitorship organizations, but if you have more priority members than parking spots available, you're asking for trouble. It's just not worth it in the long run."

Source: Dana Hines, President and CEO, Membership Consultants, St. Louis, MO. Phone (314) 771-4664. E-mail: Dana@membership-consultants.com

Gift clubs and societies should be evaluated no less than every three years.

Lightning Source UK Ltd.
Milton Keynes UK
UKOW01f0820020813

214783UK00006B/140/P